PARADOXES OF
GAMBLING BEHAVIOUR

PARADOXES OF GAMBLING BEHAVIOUR

Willem Albert Wagenaar

Professor of Experimental Psychology,
Leiden University, The Netherlands

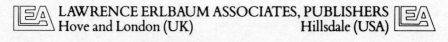 LAWRENCE ERLBAUM ASSOCIATES, PUBLISHERS
Hove and London (UK)   Hillsdale (USA)

Lawrence Erlbaum Associates Ltd., Publishers
27 Palmeira Mansions
Church Road
Hove
East Sussex, BN3 2FA
U.K.

British Library Cataloguing in Publication Data

Wagenaar, Willem A. (Willem Albert), *1941-*
    Paradoxes of gambling behaviour.
    1. Gambling. Psychological aspects
    I. Title
    157'.7

ISBN 0-86377-080-0

Printed and bound by A. Wheaton & Co. Ltd., Exeter

Contents

Foreword

This book is the fruit of many research projects, sponsored by such diverse organisations as the Office of the Public Prosecutor in The Netherlands, the Governmental Council for Casino Affairs, and the owners of various illegally operated casinos. The contribution of these sponsors was invaluable, not just for their financial support, but for opening up research opportunities that are closed to many other researchers. In most cases the aims of these projects were determined by the direct needs of the sponsors. The theoretical implications discussed in this book may come as a surprise to many of the sponsors. The applied nature of the research projects has put a limitation on the design of the experimental studies. In a casino one cannot always design experiments the way it is done in the laboratory. Still I am convinced that through the co-operation of the sponsors, it was possible to approach the experimental ideal much more closely than in many other studies published to date. The studies were executed in close co-operation with many colleagues, both at the Institute for Perception TNO, and at the Experimental Psychology Unit of Leiden University. Of all these people, I especially want to mention Gideon Keren, with whom the studies reported in Chapters 2, 3, 6, and 7 were planned and executed. A slightly different version of Chapter 7 is published as a joint paper in the *Journal of Behavioral Decision Making*. I acknowledge the experienced hand of André Huigen, who drew all the figures, and I thank Kate Hudson and the editors of Lawrence Erlbaum Associates Ltd. for their corrections of my defective usage of the English language.

CHAPTER 1

Theoretical Contexts

Two-hundred-and-fifty years ago, in 1734, the Dutch magazine *The Hollandsche Spectator* contained the following curious advertisement (Fokker, 1862):
"The publisher is requested, with permission of *The Spectator*, at the earliest possible moment to make public, that if the owner of ticket no. 1431 in the second draw of the Eleventh State Lottery, would transfer that ticket to the person in whose name this advertisement was placed, he shall receive 50 guilders. The petitioner has the firm impression that a considerable prize will fall on it. He relies upon a calculation, of which he wishes to reveal nothing more than that this number is divisible by nine and that the time letters of his name constitute the same number." (P.138)

A heated discussion immediately arose concerning the sanity of the advertiser. Two letters are memorable. In the first, the advertiser disclosed his identity: he was Conradus Leopoldus van Luckwichel (a pseudonym: wichel means divining rod; hence: the luckseeker). He defended his sanity firstly by arguing that the owner of ticket no. 1431, who had paid Dfl. 10 for it, apparently cherished a similar reasoning, because he refused to sell it for a five-fold price. But he also warned the owner that he could never profit from his property: "Because it is clear from the advertisement that only I, and no other person, will according to my reasoning, win anything of value on this lottery ticket." (P.139)

His reasoning ran as follows: "If we subtract 1431 from the year 1734, the remainder is 303. The beginning and the end of this number together make six, the first perfect number. They enclose the number zero which, having the shape of a circle, is the greatest and most perfect of all figures.... My age was 303 months, that is 25 1/4 years, on the day I submitted my request to the publisher; a circumstance that cannot be

1

without benefit." He had not paid attention to lotteries previously, because: "the time had to be right. I have just come of age, and received my capital from my guardians who, in accordance with the laudable customs of these substitute parents, supported me in such slender manner so that I was unable to wager money in lotteries, if you may call it wagering when you acquire lottery tickets the way I do."(P.139)

The second letter was from the owner of ticket no. 1431. He claimed that he did not give any credence to the prediction, nor understand its rationale. But he wanted to keep the ticket anyway, even if someone offered a hundred ducats. He explained that he was wealthy enough to afford himself the expense of a ticket, and that he did not need the 50 guilders offered by Mr. Luckwichel. He had acquired the ticket in order to have the chance of winning a fortune. Why would he now deprive himself of this opportunity? Moreover, his wife had told him: "I do not understand all these minute calculations, but this I do understand, that the lottery ticket is as good in your hands as in anyone's. It is all in the drum; will the ticket change place when you sell your receipt to someone else?"(P.140)

In her last statement she referred to the practice of mixing all lottery tickets in a large drum, out of which the winning tickets were drawn. Finally, the nephew of the owner commented that he knew two fools: "One who made so much fuss about the numbers. And one who claimed not to believe this infatuation, but proved the contrary by his behaviour." (P.140)

The story is an excellent illustration of what I mean by paradoxes of gambling behaviour. Mr. Luckwichel offered to pay for one ticket only, the amount that would have paid for five tickets in the same lottery. Apparently he was convinced that this one particular ticket was worth more than five others, and this conviction was based solely on considerations that were unrelated to the mechanical process of drawing tickets from the drum. It is not clear how the results of his cabbala could have influenced the drawing of tickets, unless it is assumed that mysterious influences, other than the actual shuffling and drawing, affect the outcome. In the following chapters we will see that many gamblers cherish similar beliefs. The discussion seems to concentrate on the question whether the ticket will be lucky, dependent on whom the owner is. Mr. Luckwichel's cabbala implies a positive answer, because it was based on his personal situation. The ticket would be lucky in his hands, not in somebody else's. Many gamblers believe that luck is personal, or even that luck is an aspect of personality, and that indeed one person's luck cannot be transferred to another person. The owner's wife thought differently. She accepted the possibility that ticket no. 1431 would be a lucky one. Therefore she agreed to keep it. But she refused to believe that luck would depend on the owner's identity, because "it is all in the drum." How then, if only physical causation determines the outcome, this ticket could be especially lucky and worth more than five other tickets, remains a puzzle. The owner's nephew adopted a third position: he did not even believe that ticket no. 1431 would be more lucky than other tickets.

The existence of organised gambling is in itself as much a paradox as the foregoing anecdote. The organisers invariably win, while the players on the whole lose. It is, of course, true that occasionally players may win, but the law of large numbers specifies that, with continued gambling, the gross result will approximate the mean expected outcome as determined by the odds of the game. In organised gambling the expected outcome is always positive for the organiser, and negative for the player. Moreover we will see that a large majority of wagers are placed by habitual gamblers, who play frequently enough to render the likelihood of overcoming the unfavourable odds infinitely small. Why does the gambling industry attract so many clients, when these same clients are certain to lose? Don't these people know that they are losing? Or do they like to lose? Do they perhaps believe that just once they are going to have a big win, and regain everything they lost before? Do they, like Conradus Leopoldus van Luckwichel, believe that something special will happen, favouring them above other players, which will invalidate the expectancy that in the long run they must lose?

EXPLANATIONS OF GAMBLING

The paradox of prolonged gambling in the face of systematic losses has been explained in many different ways. First it has been argued (cf. Vickrey, 1945; Devereaux, 1968; Hess & Diller, 1969) that gamblers value the money they expect to win more highly than the money they have already lost, and that gambling is rational in this perspective. As will be argued later on, such theories are only tenable if a major part of previous losses is discounted. Second it has been said that gambling is a form of entertainment, for which players are prepared to pay (Devereaux, 1968). Third it has been argued that gambling gives prestige to the gambler. Even the anonymous gambler could be flattered by the plush environment of casinos, the polite treatment by personnel, and all the extras bestowed on players, such as drinks, meals, and shows (cf. Zola, 1963). There is also a suggestion that deep psychological motives play a role. Examples are a need for conflict resolution (Devereaux, 1968), a need for competition and aggression (Thomas, 1901; Zola, 1963), and a need for self-punishment in neurotic people (Bergler, 1957). All these explanations could carry some truth. But none of them provides insight into the reasoning of Mr. Luckwichel and his contemporaries. Their appraisal of how lotteries operate, and how one should bet, tells a story of its own. The strong belief in principles other than statistical expectation constitutes a sufficient explanation of gambling and could, more than other explanations, provide some understanding, not only of why people gamble, but also of how people gamble.

The thesis defended throughout this monograph is that the nature of the gambling paradox is cognitive. Gamblers are motivated by a way of reasoning, not by defects of personality, education or social environment. A hint in this direction can be gained when we look at the vast number of people regularly involved in gambling. In The Netherlands 2 million people out of 14 million take part each month in the State Lottery. An even larger number play in the Giro Lottery, football pools, lotto games, foreign (especially German) lotteries, number games, illegal commercial lotteries, and semi-legal Bingo games. In addition there is betting on horses, there are four state-controlled casinos with an annual total attendance of one-and-a-half million people, and about 200 illegal casinos with a clientele of some 200,000 regular gamblers. In the United States about 60% of the population engage in some sort of gambling (cf. Lesieur & Custer, 1984). Gambling is almost universal. It cannot be explained by a defect in a minority of people.

I will attempt to support my thesis by an experimental investigation of human cognition. Often my subjects will have been observed in casinos or other gambling places. But not always because, again, it is my conviction that the cognitive factors inducing gamblers to gamble can be found in the large majority of people.

If indeed gambling should be understood in the perspective of human cognition, it may be useful to place it within the context of a theory of cognitive processes. At least two such contexts present themselves. One is the context of normative decision theory, which contains as one of its postulates that every decision problem can be modelled as a choice among gambles. The theory claims that it can predict a rational decision maker's preferences for gambles. The least such a theory should be able to do is predict gamblers' preferences for gambles unless it is claimed that 60% of the population is not rational. But in that case the theory would not have much practical value. We can smell a rat here, because in its simplest form normative decision theory predicts that gamblers will not gamble. This prediction is obviously not borne out by the facts.

The other theoretical context in which gambling behaviour can be placed is generally known as "heuristics and biases." The basic, somewhat hidden, underlying assumption is that strategies for decision making are chosen from a large and variable repertoire. The strategies are selected on the basis of similarity between the actual situation and previous situations in which a strategy worked out well. The bulk of experimental studies in this tradition attempted to demonstrate the variety of strategies in the repertoire, but little attention has been paid to the rules governing selection from the repertoire.

Both theoretical contexts have their weaknesses, and it is even questionable whether, in the end, they will help us to understand the behaviour of gamblers. But since I intend to refer to these contexts throughout the book, I will describe both of them in some detail in the following paragraphs. A discussion of their usefulness will be postponed till the last chapter, where more actual data about gambling behaviour and its paradoxes are presented.

NORMATIVE DECISION THEORY

In normative decision theory decisions are modelled as choices among altern atives. A decision to go skiing is modelled as a choice between skiing and not skiing. Decisions are usually complicated by the fact that the alternatives have uncertain outcomes. It is not certain that there will be enough snow to ski, or that you will not break your legs. There is no way to evade uncertainty completely. You cannot wait till there is more snow, without running the risk that, in fact, there will be less snow. This means that the decision must be based on expectancies. According to the theory, the expectancy related to a choice alternative consists of two elements: the utility of that alternative and an estimated probability that this utility will indeed be effectuated. These aspects are combined in some way, in order to obtain one characteristic of the attractiveness of an alternative. The combination rule is chosen such that the expected utility equals the mean utility obtained in the long run. In practice this means multiplication of probability and utility. The outcome of a gamble is a good example. Suppose that I want to decide whether I should buy a ticket in a lottery. There is only one prize of Dfl. 1000, 500 tickets are sold, and each ticket costs Dfl. 10. The outcome of not buying a ticket is clear: I keep my 10 guilders, and I will not win 1000 guilders. But the outcome of buying a ticket is more complex. The investment may yield a prize of Dfl. 1000 which amounts to a net profit of Dfl. 990. I may also just lose 10 guilders. The proposal of normative theory is that the mean result that will be achieved when the gamble is played an infinite number of times, is taken as the quantity that characterises the attractiveness of the lottery, even when the lottery is played only once. If, for sake of simplicity, we equate the utility of money to the amount of money, the mean obtained utility will be equal to the mean outcome. In the long run, if the lottery is fair, we will lose Dfl. 10 in 499 times out of 500, and win Dfl. 990 only once in 500 times. The mean result is:

$$1/500 \times 990 - 499/500 \times 10 = -Dfl.8$$

Thus the choice is between losing an average Dfl. 8, or the status quo in which nothing is lost or won. The wisdom of this reduction to long run expectancies was questioned by Lopes (1981) and Keren and Wagenaar (1987). The argument is that it is only natural for people to consider the outcomes actually possible of +990 and -10 when the gamble is a unique event. The expected outcome will in the unique case never materialise. Tversky and Bar-Hillel (1983) argued that a rational decision maker should use the long run expectancy as a decision criterion, even in the unique case. The logical reasons that support this view could appeal to some theorists, but there is of course no reason why gamblers must share this theoretical position. On the contrary, it is quite possible that gamblers, who play so often that long-term considerations will apply, do in fact consider each gamble as a separate and unique event, which is in no way related to previous or future gambles. An example may help to illustrate the point. Let us assume that a person owns Dfl. 50 after a night of gambling, but needs Dfl. 1000 to fly home. Placing the whole sum on one number of the roulette table will solve the problem in the event of a win, while the situation is not essentially worsened after a loss. Seen in the perspective of the real possible outcomes of a unique event the gamble may be acceptable. The mean outcome in the long run is a loss of Dfl. 1.35, which will not solve the problem. The long run perspective discards the solution that could be reached after one round of playing.

The model is considerably more complicated when utility and monetary value are not equated. If utility is interpreted as the subjective value attached to an amount of money, we must admit that losing Dfl. 10 means more for one person than for another. Even with one and the same person we can find that losing Dfl. 10 means more on one day than on another. Or that being cheated of Dfl.10 in a two guilders transaction means more than being cheated of Dfl. 10 in a many-thousands of guilders transaction. Let u(A) stand for the utility of an amount A. The mean utility of the results in our lottery is then expressed by:

$$1/500 \times u(990) + 499/500 \times u(-10)$$

Suppose that the utility of -10, that is the utility of losing Dfl. 10, is zero. This means that a person really does not mind losing 10 guilders. Suppose also that the utility of winning 1000 guilders is very high. In that case the expected utility of the lottery, which is, according to the theory, equal to its mean utility after an infinite number of plays, would be positive. Thus the choice is between a zero status quo (not buying a lottery ticket) and a positive expected utility of buying a ticket. This representation might lead to acceptance of the gamble.

Indeed the simplest explanation of the gambling paradox is that people use expected utility instead of expected value as a decision criterion, and that the utility of losing small amounts is neglected, compared to the utility of winning large amounts. Verification of this explanation is, of course, only possible if we can establish a relation between the value and utility of money. That is, we must measure utility.

Utilities can be measured only under some highly specific conditions, first formulated by the economists Von Neumann and Morgenstern (1944). These conditions are, in reality, hypotheses about human behaviour, and before we can undertake the measurement of utilities we should verify the correctness of these hypotheses. As said before, the normative theory of decision making represents decisions as choices among uncertain alternatives. Each alternative is decomposed into probabilities and utilities of outcomes, that is, into gambles. The validity of this approach has been challenged before by many authors (cf. Berkeley & Humphreys, 1982), mostly on the basis of gambles offered in laboratory conditions. Choices among real gambles, i.e. gambles offered by the gambling industry, have been rarely studied in relation to the Von Neumann and Morgenstern axioms. What should we think about the portrayal of decisions as choices among gambles, if we find that the conditions for measurement of utilities are not even met for real gambles? If decisions are to be modelled as gambles, it should at least be possible to model the decision to accept a gamble as a gamble.

SOME UTILITY AXIOMS

The following axioms are particularly relevant for gambling. In the discussion I will denote probabilities by p, and utilities by u.

Axiom 3, Continuity of the Scale

If we define two extreme outcomes of a lottery, like winning a million guilders, or losing everything you own in the world, we can easily set up a lottery involving these outcomes and two corresponding probabilities:

p1 to win one million guilders

p2 to lose everything you own.

Axiom 3 states that we can always find values of p1 and p2, such that the lottery involving the extreme outcomes is judged to be equally acceptable as receiving a certain prize with a utility between the utilities of the two extremes. In other words: by making a probability mixture of two extreme utilities we can reach every utility in between.

Given that a gain is always attractive, the axiom states that a chance of experiencing an extreme loss can be compensated for by the prospect of a large benefit, no matter how unlikely this prospect is. One should be able to name a prize A at which the following lottery would become attractive:

p1 = 0.001 to win A

p2 = 0.999 to lose everything you own.

This axiom is really intriguing. On the one hand the lottery looks utterly unattractive, because in practice one can be certain of losing. On the other hand we know that this is exactly what happens so often in casinos: people are prepared to put their full income and more at stake, despite the bleak prospect of ever winning a fortune. If such morbid gambling looks alien to us, could the reason be that compulsive gamblers obey the third axiom, whereas we do not?

The axiom is called continuity of the scale, because it ensures that each point on the utility scale can be reached through the combination of extreme consequences. No negative outcome is so bad that it falls outside the range where compensation by positive outcomes is still possible. This is the very assumption which is, nowadays, challenged when cost-benefit analyses of large-scale technologies are discussed. In the analysis of the decision to build a nuclear reactor the costs of an accident are compared to the benefits of energy production. Opponents would argue that these matters are not on one common scale. An accident can be so devastating in terms of loss of lives and infliction of misery, that it cannot be compensated for by any prospect of profit or welfare. Gamblers do not consider their losses to be so devastating, or at least organised gambling does not encourage them to look on their losses as devastating. Hence, although we must assume that in reality many people will violate axiom 3 when extreme consequences are involved, we must fear that habitual gamblers behave in accordance with the axiom across a large range of monetary values.

Axiom 5, Substitution

Ten tickets, numbered from one to ten, are thrown in a hat. One ticket is drawn randomly. If a ticket with a number from one to nine is drawn, you receive Dfl. 100. If the ticket with number ten is drawn you receive nothing. The expected monetary outcome of the lottery equals :

$$0.9 \times 100 + 0.1 \times 0 = \text{Dfl.}90$$

The expected utility is computed by:

$$0.9 \times u(100) + 0.1 \times u(0)$$

The substitution axiom states that gambles can be replaced by their expected utility. Thus people should be indifferent when facing the choice between playing the lottery or receiving as a certain outcome a sum with the same utility. Kahneman and Tversky (1979) demonstrated that a large majority of people prefer the certain reception of Dfl. 90 to the lottery outlined above. Assuming that u (0) = 0, this so-called certainty effect could signify that

$$0.9 \times u(100) < u(90), \text{ or that } u(100)/u(90) < 1.0/0.9$$

Within the framework of the expected utility model the certainty effect implies that the utility curve for profits is concave. Another explanation is that people would feel extremely silly after losing a certain profit, which means that the zero outcome has an extra negative utility.

We can also construct a gamble in which there are nine chances of losing Dfl. 100, and one chance of losing nothing. In that case it seems that people prefer the gamble to a certain loss of Dfl. 90. This so-called reflection effect may signify that

$$0.9 \times u(-100) > u(-90)$$

or that the utility curve for losses is convex. Again there is another possible explanation, viz. that the feeling "At least I tried" adds a positive utility to the gamble, whatever its outcome. The certainty effect and the reflection effect were both used by Kahneman and Tversky as a demonstration of the non-linearity of utility curves, but they also could be taken as a demonstration of the fact that gambling itself has a non-zero utility. This would be a violation of axiom 5, because substitution of a gamble by a certain outcome would do away with this utility of gambling. The sign of the utility of gambling may vary with the form of the bet, but also with the intentions of the decision maker. It is not unreasonable to assume that gamblers have on the whole a positive utility of gambling. Gamblers seek the thrill of uncertainty, and their problem might well be that the positive utility of gambling compensates for the negative utility of losing money. The substitution axiom is clearly violated by all those gamblers who prefer to play a full night till they are broke, rather than paying all their money at the casino entrance and going home immediately.

Substitution also plays a role in the following problem. Assume again a lottery with nine chances of winning Dfl. 100, and one chance of winning nothing. In line with the certainty effect many people are prepared to sell the right of playing in this lottery for an amount less than the expected monetary outcome of Dfl. 90. Let us assume that some people are prepared to sell this right for Dfl. 60. Then there is an equivalence of:

B1 9 chances of winning Dfl. 100
     1 chance of winning nothing
B2 10 chances of winning Dfl. 60
Now we add to B1 another set B3 of 90 chances of winning nothing:
B1 + B3 9 chances of winning Dfl. 100
          91 chances of winning nothing.
Since B2 is equivalent to B1, we may, according to the axiom, substitute the one for the other, and obtain an equally attractive result:
B2 + B3 10 chances of winning Dfl. 60
          90 chances of winning nothing.
The French economist Allais (1953) showed that the equivalence of B1 and B2 is disrupted by the addition of B3. When the certainty of B2 is no longer present, people seem to concentrate on the bigger prize, even if the chances are somewhat slimmer. Allais' paradox shows that "playing safe," even when it is preferred in cases where chances of winning are high, may disappear when the chance of winning becomes very remote. People who do not normally take risks could, once they are confronted with an unattractive set of gambles, lose part or all of their risk aversion. This situation occurs when the choice is between a small and an even smaller probability of ever winning back your losses, which is often encountered in the casino.

Axiom 4, Monotonicity of the Scale

The impossibility of substituting a certain outcome for a gamble also interferes with axiom 4. Assume three prizes in a lottery: Dfl. 1000, Dfl. 100, and Dfl. 10. It is only plausible that one would prefer Dfl. 1000 to Dfl. 100, and Dfl. 100 to Dfl.10. Hence the utilities of these amounts have the same order as their monetary values. If this is so, one should not prefer option B2 in the following example:
B1 win Dfl. 1000 for sure
B2 p1 to win Dfl. 100
     p2 to win Dfl. 10
The expected utility of option B2 lies always between the utilities of 10 and 100 guilders. The monotonicity requirement states that nowhere between those utilities can there be a utility that surpasses the utility of Dfl. 1000.

Habitual gamblers seem to violate this axiom frequently. The majority of gamblers interviewed by us visit casinos three or four nights a week. They have done so for years and without exception they agree that they lose in the long run. In a computer simulation of the game of blackjack, which will be presented in Chapter 2, we found that coming out ahead after 50,000 hands, which is about the number of hands an habitual player can play in a year, has a probability of far less than one in 100,000. Therefore all habitual blackjack players must expect to lose a little in one month, and a lot in another month. In a sense they are confronted with the options: not to play, and lose nothing; to play, and lose a little; or to play, and lose a lot. Axiom 4 states that no combination of the second and third option should be more attractive than to lose nothing, unless losing a little is seen as more attractive than not losing at all. Since gamblers almost unanimously declare that they hate to lose, they should in the long run decide to quit gambling. Why don't they?

The reason could be that gambling has a positive utility. The placement of utilities of certain outcomes and utilities of gambles along the same scale leads to a violation of axiom 4, unless the utility of gambling itself is taken into account.

Axiom 6, Compound Lotteries

A non-zero utility of gambling would also cause a violation of the sixth axiom. One may organise a lottery, in which the prize is a ticket for another lottery. This happens, for instance, in French Roulette. If Dfl. 10 is placed on red, and zero appears, the bet is not immediately lost, but kept "in prison" for one round. If the next outcome is red the bet is returned, if it is black the bet is lost. In the case of another zero the bet stays in prison. Since finally the likelihoods of leaving prison after red or after black are equal, the structure of the bet looks like:

$p1 = 18/37$ to win Dfl. 10
$p2 = 18/37$ to lose Dfl. 10
$p3 = 1/37$ to stay in prison,
then $p4 = 1/2$ to win nothing
    $p5 = 1/2$ to lose Dfl. 10.

Axiom 6 states that this compound bet is equivalent to the simple bet:

$p6 = 18/37$ to win Dfl. 10
$p7 = 1/37 \times 1/2 = 1/74$ to win nothing
$p8 = 18/37 + 1/37 \times 1/2 = 1/2$ to lose Dfl. 10.

Reduction of compound lotteries to simple ones is not the same as substitution of certain outcomes for bets, because the gambling aspect is preserved.

Another example. Suppose that someone wins a blackjack hand, and that the probability of winning was $1/2$. In the next round he bets the original bet of Dfl. 10, plus the amount won. Suppose that the probability of winning is again $1/2$. The two successive bets can be charted as follows:

$p1 = 1/2$ to lose Dfl. 10
$p2 = 1/2$ to win Dfl. 10,
then $p3 = 1/2$ to lose Dfl. 20
    $p4 = 1/2$ to win Dfl. 20.

According to axiom 6 this can be reduced to the simple lottery:

$p5 = 3/4$ to lose Dfl. 10
$p6 = 1/4$ to win Dfl. 30.

It is easy to see that we can combine all successive rounds played on a night in the casino into one equivalent multi-alternative lottery, and that is where the weakness of the axiom lies. To casino visitors one night of playing, ending with a loss of Dfl. 1000, is not the same as one minute of playing, resulting in the same loss. The amusement of one night might be worth the investment, whereas just one minute of playing is not. Players could already have tacitly accepted that they will lose Dfl. 1000, and still have the goal of holding onto Dfl. 1000 for as long as possible. Reduction of the compound to the simple takes away this challenge.

EVALUATION OF THE CONTEXT OF NORMATIVE THEORY

The acceptance of gambles with a negative expected value can only be explained within the framework of a normative theory when it is assumed that utility and monetary value are not identical. This introduces the problem that utility, being a subjective quantity, must be measured independently of value. Measurement of utility is only possible when people conform to rules such as the ones specified by the Von Neumann and Morgenstern axioms. It is obvious that gamblers violate some of these axioms. This does not mean that the normative theory is wrong, as it was not meant to explain, predict or describe actual human behaviour. Its main use is as a yardstick, that measures the extent to which choices are accomplishing the maximum utility in the long run. However, when gamblers violate the utility axioms, utility theory can no longer be used as a meaningful context within which to understand the reasoning of gamblers. When the utility of outcomes cannot be measured, we cannot decide whether these outcomes are in any sense optimal. As a consequence I will not, throughout this book, refer to the normative theory as an explanatory, predictive or descriptive context. The concept of expected value (not expected utility) will be invoked occasionally, but only as a quantification of long-term profits and losses related to games or strategies.

There remains the more encompassing question of what we must think about the reduction of decision problems to choices among gambles, when the theory cannot be applied to real gambles. Opponents of normative theories have argued that people do not base their decisions on an evaluation of probabilities and utilities. Instead it is assumed that a large repertoire of reasoning strategies is employed, and that these strategies are based on experience, not on principles of rationality.

Normative theory reduces decision making to gambling. If we are forced to conclude that the utility axioms are violated by gamblers, we may do just the reverse. We may ask whether strategies, heuristics or ways of thinking which are used by people in everyday decision making are also found in the large population of gamblers.

HEURISTICS AND BIASES

The theoretical context of the "heuristics and biases" tradition is weak. The body of evidence consists of a large set of experimental demonstrations. The experiments identify heuristics employed in everyday problem solving, and demonstrate that in some well-chosen conditions the same heuristics may lead to sub-optimal, or even absurd outcomes.

An example is the availability heuristic (Tversky & Kahneman, 1973): what comes first to mind is judged to be more likely. The probability of being highjacked in an airplane, or being killed through terrorist action, is estimated to be higher than the probability of being the victim of criminal assault in your own neighbourhood, simply because more publicity is given to terrorism. This may, in the summer of 1986, have caused many Americans to spend the summer in the U.S.A., not in Europe. In fact the probability of being killed through criminal action was much higher in the U.S.A. The availability heuristic caused people to prefer the more dangerous option.

In the same vein it is possible to increase the subjective probability of winning in lotteries and other gambles, simply by making the winning highly available. The winners are shown on television; the number of prizes is widely advertised, while the number of non-wins is not; slot machines are grouped together in sets of hundreds, such that the rattling of money is heard continuously. In a more subtle way it is possible that gamblers suppress the memory of losing. It has been found that good memories are more available than bad memories (cf. Wagenaar, 1986), which would cause gamblers to overestimate the probability of winning.

Another example is the neglect of base rates. When given information about a student's personality, one might conclude that he is studying library sciences rather than engineering, just on the basis of a stereotyped view of these professions, and neglecting the vastly differing base rates. Gamblers could, by the same neglect of base rates, cherish strong beliefs that tonight will be their lucky night, in which they will make up for all their previous losses.

There is an ongoing discussion about the question of to what extent people follow heuristics and biases when making important decisions in everyday life (cf. the symposium on the validity of studies on heuristics and biases in Humphreys, Svenson & Vári, 1983). An extremely interesting book by Dixon (1976) analysed heuristics and biases in military decision making. A closer study of gambling could add to this discussion, in as far as gambling can be accepted as a normal daily activity. At least we can say that there are more gamblers than military. In Chapter 8 we will have more to say about this issue. At this moment it suffices to underline that, compared to the situations studied within the context of heuristics and biases, the gambling situation has at least three distinct advantages.

The first advantage is that gambling problems are naturally presented in a quantitative manner. Unlike problems used in some of the traditional laboratory experiments, the problem definition in terms of probabilities and monetary outcomes is accepted as perfectly normal by all participants. The large majority of gamblers have so much experience that their sub-optimal or even outrageous decisions cannot simply be attributed to an unusual or incomprehensible problem representation. Neither can it be argued that extension of the observation period would reveal a gradual adaptation to the experimental conditions.

Secondly, one is assured that participants are intensely interested in the outcomes of their decisions. Some of the traditional heuristics and biases results have been undermined by the assumption that subjects were not really interested, because the problems were too abstract. Gamblers risk large sums of money, amounts that surpass any level of incentives that could ever be used in laboratory experiments, and it is not reasonable to assume that players would not be interested in the outcomes.

In the third place gambling allows for the collection of many replications within subjects. Gamblers who continue their play of roulette or blackjack for a full evening make hundreds of decisions, and many of these under similar circumstances.

Evaluation of the Heuristics and Biases Context

The weakness of the heuristics and biases concept is that the conditions that evoke the various strategies are not well specified. Explanations of behaviour by a matching heuristic from the extensive repertoire are mostly *post hoc*. The list of heuristics presented by Hogarth (1981) is so long that it seems impossible to imagine behaviours that cannot be understood in the context of at least one of them. Two fully opposing behaviours can still be in accordance with one of the heuristics from Hogarth's list.

As an example of the problem we will look at the selection of bet sizes after winning and losing. There exists a heuristic called "representativeness," which specifies that people expect small samples to be representative of population parameters. When in a game there is a 50% chance of winning, people expect that a small number of rounds will also reflect this even chance. This is only possible when runs of gains and losses are short: a run of six losses in a row would upset the local representativeness. This mechanism may explain the well-known gamblers fallacy: the expectation that the probability of winning increases with the length of an ongoing run of losses. The representativeness heuristic predicts that players will increase their bet after a run of losses, and decrease it after a run of gains. This is indeed what about half of the players at blackjack tables do (cf. Chapter 2). But the other half show the reverse behaviour: they increase their bets after winning, and decrease them after losing, which is predicted by the availability heuristic. After a run of losses, losing becomes the better available outcome, which may cause an overestimation of the probability of losing. When we exclude the use of betting systems such as discussed in Chapter 4, the repertoire of heuristics predicts both an increase and decrease of bet size after losing, and without further indications about conditions that determine preferences for heuristics, the whole theoretical context will be destined to provide explanations on the basis of hindsight only.

Experiments on heuristics and biases tend to take the character of demonstrations rather than tests. Each of the classical papers summarised by Tversky and Kahneman (1974) contains a number of situations in which the heuristic was seemingly applied. But the set of situations is composed selectively, based on the fine intuition of the experimenters and on the occurrence of the predicted phenomena. A real test of validity of an heuristic can only be made when it is first defined under what conditions the heuristic will be and will not be used. Subsequently, experimental situations should be selected from both sets, and the prediction about occurrence and non-occurrence of the heuristic tested. Such a design will allow the prediction of heuristics that *will* be used. In contrast, the demonstrations provided thus far can only tell us what heuristics *may* be used.

PLAN OF THIS BOOK

From the foregoing discussion it is clear that both theoretical contexts have their weaknesses. A closer analysis of these theories, and the extent to which they help us to understand the paradoxes of gambling behaviour will be postponed to Chapter 8. First, I will present observations on the game of blackjack (Chapters 2 and 3), on roulette (Chapter 4), and on lotteries (Chapter 5). In Chapters 6 and 7, I will provide some observations and thoughts about the distinction between chance and skill, and chance and luck. Both skill and luck are extremely important concepts, even when the outcome of a game is, in fact, fully dependent on chance. The reason is that players may attach much weight to their skills, or to the influence of luck, thereby neglecting the base rates determined by the statistical principles underlying the game.

Only in Chapter 8 will I re-examine the theoretical discussion introduced in this chapter.Gambling is a paradox in itself, because those who engage in it most frequently must have experienced that they lose most of the time. Gamblers must have strong beliefs that things will turn out otherwise, that for once statistical rules will not apply, or that they possess an extraordinary gift that will help them to overcome the odds. But, as revealed by the example of Mr. Luckwichel's advertisement, such beliefs add to the paradoxical nature of gambling, rather than reducing it. It is not the purpose of this book to resolve these paradoxes. But the closer study of them may provide some insights in human cognition, that can also be applied in other areas of psychological research. Gambling is not the only paradox of human behaviour. It will be useful to investigate what gambling can tell us about those other paradoxes.

CHAPTER 2

Blackjack: The Game Players Refuse to Win

Among the many casino games blackjack is the only one with a positive expected value for the players. That is, provided that the players follow the optimal strategy, they should be able to win in the long run. The paradoxical character of this statement is obvious when one realises that no commercial casino will continue to offer a game at which players win consistently. From the fact that blackjack *is* offered in numerous casinos all around the world, it can be concluded that players do not win. In my nightly discussions with many habitual blackjack players I discovered that they do not follow the optimal strategy, mainly because they refuse to believe that the strategy is optimal. It is, of course, also a matter of investing some effort in the learning phase, but such an investment is small in comparison to what blackjack players who play three nights a week throughout the year, are prepared to lose. The obstacle is not the difficult theory underlying the optimal strategy, but, as we will see in a later chapter, the presence of conflicting theories, held by a large majority of gamblers, and leading to sub-optimal behaviour.

In the present chapter I will present studies on the behaviour of blackjack players, in the natural setting of three Dutch State Casinos, and an Amsterdam underground casino. Most of the players were not aware of the fact that they were being observed, the others did not object to our presence, if we could convince them that we were not tax inspectors. The exceptional feature of this study is that we were able to study gamblers for hours in succession, making complete records of their decisions and the outcomes of their gambles. This is exceptional because in all casinos around the world it is forbidden to make notes at the blackjack tables. The reason is, as we will see, that recording previous outcomes is the key element of any winning strategy. This is in contrast with roulette, where the casinos stimulate the recording of previous outcomes, because it enhances the suggestion that skill might do some good. In fact there is no useful information to be obtained. The only other study of blackjack players in a natural setting is by Bond (1974) who observed players during a small number of rounds, and went subsequently to the men's rooms to write down the record from memory. The reason that my colleagues and I were permitted to make complete records is that the casinos needed these data for legal and management reasons. The two studies reported in this chapter were executed in close co-operation with my colleague Gideon Keren, and have been published before in a different form (Keren & Wagenaar, 1983; Keren & Wagenaar, 1985).

THE GAME OF BLACKJACK

In order to appreciate the following discussion it is necessary to understand some fundamental rules of blackjack. The rules given here are for the game as played in the casinos where the observations were collected. Other casinos may use slightly different rules and procedures. For more detailed descriptions see Epstein (1967), Griffin (1979), Humble and Cooper (1980), Revere (1980), Thorp (1966), and Wong (1975).

A blackjack game has a dealer (representing the house) and between one and seven players. Four ordinary 52-card decks are shuffled together and placed in a card-holding device called a *shoe*. A plastic card is inserted at approximately three-quarters of the way through the shoe (i.e., after approximately three packs, or 156 cards). Whenever the plastic card is reached, all the cards are reshuffled before the game continues.

The players place all bets except insurance (discussed later) before any cards are dealt. Each player has a box in which bets are placed and the casino establishes a minimum and maximum bet per box. After bets have been placed, the dealer deals two cards to each player and a single card to the dealer (called dealer's *upcard*), all cards being dealt face up. The numerical value of each card is simply its face value except for the picture cards all of which have a value of 10. The player can choose either 1 or 11 as the value of an ace. A hand containing an ace that can be counted as 11 without causing the total of the hand to exceed 21 is termed a *soft* hand (e.g., ace and 6 is called a soft 17). All other hands are called *hard* hands. The object of each player is to obtain a total greater than that of the dealer but not exceeding 21. If the first two cards dealt to either the player or the dealer consist of an ace and a 10-value card they constitute a *blackjack* or natural; this is the best hand and beats any other hand, including any other combination which totals 21. The player who gets a blackjack wins 1.5 times the original bet unless the dealer also gets a blackjack, in which case the game is considered a draw and no money changes hands.

After the initial cards have been dealt, the players have an opportunity to draw additional cards. Proceeding clockwise, each player in turn may either *stand* (draw no additional cards) or *hit* (request additional cards from the dealer). These are dealt face up, one at a time. If the player *busts*, that is, the total value of the hand exceeds 21, the bet is lost to the dealer who then proceeds to the next player. After all players have finished drawing cards the dealer deals cards to the dealer's hand. As long as the dealer's total is 16 or less an additional card must be dealt. If the dealer's total is 17 or more, the dealer must stand. If the dealer busts (exceeds 21), all remaining players (those who did not bust) win an amount equal to their original bet. If neither dealer nor player busts, the dealer collects the bet of any player whose total is less than the dealer's total and pays an amount equal to the original bet to any player whose total exceeds the dealer's total. In a tie between dealer and player, no money changes hands.

Under certain circumstances, three additional options are available to the player:

Splitting pairs: If the first two cards dealt to the player have identical numerical values (e.g., 6,6) the player may split the pair, place the value of the original bet on each of the two new hands, and then proceed as usual, playing each hand separately.

Doubling: If the first two cards dealt to the player total 9, 10, or 11, the player has the option to *double down*, in which case the initial bet is doubled and just one additional card is drawn.

Insurance: If the dealer's upcard (first card) is an ace, each player may place an additional side bet (not more than half the original bet) that the dealer will end up with a blackjack, that is, receive a 10 as second card. If the dealer does indeed receive a 10, the player wins twice the amount of the side bet. Otherwise, the side bet is lost to the dealer.

POSSIBLE STRATEGIES IN BLACKJACK

Never Bust

Unlike roulette, blackjack offers the players an opportunity to influence their expected outcome. This is already obvious if one realises that blackjack players can deliberately ruin themselves by continuing to hit until the hand busts. In roulette it is impossible to lose a bet at will.

In order to evaluate some possible strategies for the player, we constructed a computer simulation based on the rules described. The outcome of each strategy was evaluated on the basis of a simulation of 1,000,000 players' hands. The simulation assumes seven players; consequently, the number of dealer's hands is approximately one-seventh of a million.

Blackjack does not constitute a game in the usual sense of game theory, because the dealer's strategy is fixed. The dealer does not make any decisions nor react to the strategies or results of the players. The biggest advantage of the dealer over the players stems from the fact that, whenever both the player and the dealer bust, the player's bet is lost. A simple strategy some players employ is called *never bust*. The strategy consists of hitting at 11 points, and standing at a hard total of 12 points. Thus the situation in which both player and dealer bust is avoided. The dealer's advantage is however now exchanged for the disadvantage of frequent standing at a number below 17. Such a hand can only be won when the dealer busts, because the dealer must hit at a total below 17. Our simulation showed that in the long run *never bust* results in an expected loss of 8% of the total investment. By this we mean that after playing 100 rounds with bets of size b, 46 hands are won and 54 are lost, so that 8b will be lost to the casino. This result is rather poor compared, for instance, to the expected loss in roulette, which is only 2.7%.

Mimic the Dealer

It can be shown that the dealer's stand/hit rule is optimal, provided that nothing is known beyond the base rate of the deck composition. The rationale for *mimic the dealer* is that "if it is good for the dealer it must also be good for the player." Because the odds of player and dealer holding any final hand value are the same, the game appears to be even. But, the player must always hit or stand first and thus always loses when player's hand busts (even when the dealer busts later on). This asymmetry in busting favours the dealer and consequently a player who mimics the dealer ends up with a negative expected value of approximately 6%.

Basic Strategy

Never bust and *mimic the dealer* use as an input only the total of the player's hand. The strategy called *Basic* also uses the dealer's upcard. It is based upon a computation of the expected value of both possible actions (e.g., hit vs. stand, split vs. not split), for every possible decision (e.g., Epstein, 1967). The action with the higher expected value belongs to the prescribed strategy.

The dealer's hand has only 10 possible values, 2 through ace (all face cards count as 10). However, the player's hand at the moment of decision could contain any of hundreds of distinct card combinations. This number of possibilities is greatly reduced by considering only the total of the player's hand. Thus, the six-card hand, 2, 2, 2, 3, 4, and 5 is strategically equivalent, in Basic, to the two-card hand 8 and 10, because both total 18.

Basic can be described by three matrices. The 10 columns of each matrix represent the dealer's upcard, 2 through ace. The rows of the three matrices represent the player's total for hard non-pair hands, for soft hands, and for pairs.

Each cell of the matrices specifies the action the Basic player should always take in that situation: stand, hit, double, or split (Basic players never buy insurance). Figure 2.1 shows the first of these matrices. The mnemonic used to remember the correct actions is very simple. Below 12 one hits or doubles. Always double against 3, 4, 5, or 6 when you can, never double against an ace. When the dealer starts with a bad upcard (2 to 6), the player should expect the dealer to bust. Therefore the player's best strategy is *never bust*. When the dealer's upcard is good (7 or above) the dealer is expected to end with a good total. Then the player's best strategy is *mimic the dealer*. The only exception is the situation in which the dealer's hand shows 2 or 3, and the player has 12 points. In a similar way the other matrices can easily be committed to memory with a minimum of effort. Complete Basic tables are presented by Braun (1980), Humble

DEALERS UPCARD

		2	3	4	5	6	7	8	9	10	A
	8	H	H	H	H	H	H	H	H	H	H
	9	H	D	D	D	D	H	H	H	H	H
10		D	D	D	D	D	D	D	D	H	H
11		D	D	D	D	D	D	D	D	D	H
12		H	H	S	S	S	H	H	H	H	H
13		S	S	S	S	S	H	H	H	H	H
14		S	S	S	S	S	H	H	H	H	H
15		S	S	S	S	S	H	H	H	H	H
16		S	S	S	S	S	H	H	H	H	H
17		S	S	S	S	S	S	S	S	S	S

(left labels: PLAYERS TOTAL)

FIG. 2.1 Hitting, standing and doubling for hard non-pair hands, according to Basic (H = hit, S = stand, D = double).

and Cooper (1980), and Thorp (1966). Playing according to Basic reduces the negative expected value to merely 0.4% of the total investment, which is very good compared to the loss of 2.7% in roulette.

Counting

An important feature of blackjack is that the cards dealt on one round are not immediately returned to the shoe but are instead put aside. Consequently, the situation is one of sampling without replacement. A player who follows a counting strategy is called a *counter* and may take advantage of this situation by keeping track of the cards that have been dealt, thus obtaining information about the cards remaining in the shoe. Most counters do not memorise every card dealt; simplifying methods have been developed in which a count of certain cards is continuously updated (mainly several versions that calculate the relative ratio of 10-value cards vs. other cards remaining in the shoe) and provide the player with important information about probabilities. Unless all the cards are reshuffled after every round (which is almost like sampling with replacement), the counter will always obtain some advantage from a counting strategy.

How does the counter utilise the information about probabilities obtained from counting? First, the Basic tables described earlier are slightly altered depending on the current count. More important, however, the current count determines whether the situation is slightly in favour of the player or in favour of the casino. The counter will place a high bet whenever the count is favourable to the players and a low bet (usually the minimum required by the casino) whenever the count is unfavourable. An example from Thorp (1966, p. 43) will clarify how a favourable or unfavourable situation may develop. Suppose that by using a single well-shuffled 52-card deck, all four aces appear on the first round. After the first round is over, the used cards are placed aside and the second round is dealt from the remaining cards. Because on the second round no aces can appear, there will be no blackjacks, no soft hands, and no splitting of aces, all of which would be advantageous to the player. Consequently, the lack of aces creates conditions unfavourable for the player, and the counter who is aware of this will place only the minimum bet. On the other hand, assume a deck that is almost depleted, in which the only cards left are a few low-value cards (2s and 3s) and a relatively large number of 10s. Such conditions are favourable for players because they will always stand whenever the total of their hand is 12 or more, owing to the high probability of the next card being a 10 leading to a bust. The dealer, who has to follow a deterministic algorithm, cannot stand with less than 17 and consequently has a high likelihood of busting. Here, the player has a higher probability of winning and the counter who is aware of this situation may take advantage of it by placing high bets.

In summary, the major advantage of counting lies in variation of bet size depending on whether the count is favourable or unfavourable. In addition, the counter uses decision rules that differ slightly from Basic, as indicated by the count. Depending on the particular rules of the casino and the specific counting method used, the counter has a positive expected value between approximately 0.5% and 2.0%.

Counting is not illegal, and one would expect many players to do it. In reality the number of proficient counters is very small. One reason could be that although the expected value is positive, the variance of the outcome is quite high, even for an extended series of hands. The standard deviation around the expected value is

$$1/\sqrt{N} \ (N = \text{number of hands played})$$

for all strategies. If 100 hands are played in one hour, which is a high speed for a full table, one working day of eight hours would result in a standard deviation of 3.5%. With an expected value of 1.5% the probability of ending with a loss after eight hours of counting would still be 33%. A chance of 99% of ending with a profit can only be expected after some 24,000 hands, or 30 days. When, due to the rules of the casino, the expected value is only +0.5%, 270 days of eight hours playing are needed to secure a profit.

The strategies can be divided over three levels. In level 1 strategies decisions are based only on one piece of information: player's total. Examples are *never bust* and *mimic the dealer*. In level 2 strategies two pieces of information are used: player's total and dealer's upcard. Examples are *Basic* and approximations of it such as will be discussed in the next section. Level 3 strategies employ, besides player's total and dealer's upcard, information about the cards that have already been played. All counting methods belong to this group.

Counting cards as a profession is hard work but will be profitable in the long run, provided that one does it long enough. Many players do not play enough hands in a year to live on card counting. But that does not explain why they do not adopt a counting strategy, or even the much simpler Basic strategy. For any number of hands the more complex strategies promise a better outcome, and one may wonder what reasons players have to believe otherwise. This question will be postponed to a later chapter, because I will first concentrate on a quantitative description of what blackjack players do.

BASIC OR NOT BASIC

The question addressed in this section is to what extent players in casinos apply the rules of Basic. In one previous study, Bond (1974) concluded that blackjack players do roughly apply Basic rules. This conclusion may be the result of the small number of observations per player. It is quite possible to play more than five hands without encountering situations in which Basic prescribes a choice that is different from, for instance, *mimic the dealer*.

In another investigation, Abram (1981) reported a small proportion: 25% of the players he observed used Basic rules. However, this number may still be an over-estimate, since the periods of observation were again very short. Moreover this study was funded by the Hotel Casino Association in Atlantic City, a group representing the interests of casino owners in a legal battle against card counters. The Association had good reasons for giving a biased picture of the ingenuity of players. If it is true that all players follow the rules of Basic, it would follow that the house does not win more than 0.5% of the bets placed on the blackjack tables. However, as we found in the Dutch State Casinos, 2.93% of the total amount of money placed on the tables is won by the house (Wagenaar & Keren, 1983). This observation was based on 101 hours, in which 30,198 hands were played. The standard deviation of the estimated win percentage is therefore

$$1/\sqrt{30198} = 0.6\%$$

Hence, Bond's conclusion cannot be true for Dutch casinos, and probably also not for other casinos, as a win percentage of 0.5 is not enough to pay the cost of running a casino. The 95% confidence interval of the estimated profit runs from 1.79% to 4.06%. If it is true that 25% of the players play Basic and 75% *mimic the dealer* (or something close to it) the house should win 4.67%, which is outside our confidence interval. Hence Abram's conclusion can also not be true for Dutch casinos.

Because of the inconclusiveness of previous studies we decided to collect some more data (cf. Keren & Wagenaar, 1983). We observed 574 players, distributed over three casinos. The players were randomly selected at all times of the day, and on all days of the week. Each observation lasted 30 hands in succession for all players, which equals 35 to 60 minutes of playing time. The exact pattern of violations will be presented in the following pages. At this moment I want to consider only the overall result, which is presented in Table 2.1.

In this table, standing at 12 when the dealer has a 2 or a 3 was not counted as a violation because its effect on expected value can be ignored. The results show that no

TABLE 2.1
Number of Violations of Basic During
30 Rounds (N=574)

No. of Violations	% of Players	No. of Violations	% of Players
0	3.8	7	9.7
1	7.2	8	6.2
2	9.2	9	5.1
3	14.3	10	2.8
4	15.1	11	2.3
5	12.4	12	2.3
6	9.7	13	0.0

more than 3.8% of the players follow Basic perfectly. The others may have an intuitive appreciation of the Basic strategy, but do not apply it as a formalism. The modal player violates Basic on one out of eight hands. This number is easier put in perspective if one realises that 60% of the players' initial two-card combination requires a decision in which Basic could be violated. The probabilities of encountering such decisions 0, 1, 2 or 3 times in 30 rounds are, respectively, 1×10^{-12}, 5×10^{-11}, 1×10^{-9}, and 2×10^{-8}. Hence the observations cannot be the result of not encountering enough decision situations in 30 rounds. The probability that Basic prescribes for a two-card combination a different choice to that of *mimic the dealer* is 25%. The probabilities of encountering this situation 0, 1, 2, or 3 times in 30 rounds are 2×10^{-4}, 0.0018, 0.0086, and 0.0269 respectively. Consequently neither can the results in Table 2.1 be explained by the fact that players did not encounter enough critical situations. Apparently players learned to do better than *mimic the dealer*, although they hardly ever obey the rules of Basic completely. If we want to find out what they are actually doing, we need a more elaborate record of all players' decisions during extended periods of observation. This is what we attempted to achieve in the following study.

EXTENSIVE STUDY OF 112 PLAYERS

Method

Unobtrusive observations were made in a small casino in Amsterdam. For each of 112 players we recorded the entire game, that is, bets placed by the player, player's and dealer's cards, and all the decisions reached by the player.

We followed a random procedure of sampling players within the constraints imposed by the environment. On each observation day, the observer first chose at random one of the tables and then three boxes out of seven on the chosen table. There were two types of tables with a minimum bet of 5 and 10 Dutch guilders, respectively. An approximately equal number of players was sampled from each type of table and from each of the seven positions at a table. The observers were quite visible, but the players did not know which of them were actually observed. The number of hands (rounds) recorded for each player varied because we had no control over the length of stay of each player. Players who did not complete at least 20 hands were discarded from the sample. The number of hands recorded for each player retained in the final sample of 112, ranged from 20 to 627 hands. Median number of observations per player was 74 hands. Median number of rounds played per hour was approximately 70, and the total number of recorded hands exceeded 11,000. Observations were made on different days of the week and at various times of the day.

Data Analysis and Interpretation

In order to analyse and evaluate the data, we used the Basic strategy as a baseline against which to compare the performance of the 112 players in our sample. Figure 2.2 presents the number of times players violated Basic relative to the frequency of occurrence of such hands. The matrix provides the data for players' hard (non-pair) hands containing 12 to 17 points and is based on 5853 observations. The cells in which a player's total is less than 12 or exceeds 17 have been omitted because players always hit when their total was below 12, and always stood with a total over 17. The number of observations per cell ranged from 62 to 109, except for the cells in which the dealer's upcard value was 10; for those cells the range was 366 to 411. Some hands appear in Fig. 2.2 more than once. For instance, a player with a total of 12 may hit and get a 2, and so the player has to decide again whether to hit or stand. The underlined numbers represent dealer-player combinations for which the Basic player should have drawn an additional card, that is, hit. The numbers in these cells are the percentages in which players failed to hit.

DEALERS UPCARD

		2	3	4	5	6	7	8	9	10	A
	12	14.5	33.7	47.7	44.1	29.9	9.4	9.0	9.3	7.7	3.7
	13	49.5	32.3	17.4	8.2	8.2	28.2	22.5	17.6	17.8	8.3
PLAYERS TOTAL	14	24.5	10.4	4.0	1.3	4.8	35.7	38.1	39.1	47.4	27.8
	15	6.3	3.6	2.5	4.1	3.5	77.6	78.4	63.9	71.5	48.1
	16	3.0	0	0	0	0	89.7	86.2	82.8	89.6	71.6
	17	0	0	0	0	0	0	1.2	0	0.5	1.2

FIG. 2.2 Percentage of decisions that violate Basic for hard non-pair hands. The underlined figures are those in which the player following Basic is required to hit. In the other cells Basic players will stand (cf. Fig. 2.1).

Subtraction of those numbers from 100 will yield the percentage of correct hits. When figures are not underlined, the player following Basic is supposed to stand, and the numbers represent the percentage of incorrect hits.

Two important findings emerge from Fig. 2.2. First, the average frequency of violations of Basic in the underlined area is considerably larger than in the non-underlined area. In other words, the percentage of cases in which players fail to draw an additional card (43.8% for hard hands) is much larger than the percentage in which they fail to stand (15.8%). This conservatism probably reflects players' fear of busting (exceeding 21). The *never bust* strategy discussed earlier is an extreme version of conservatism. Though none of the players in our sample followed that strategy strictly, many tended to play in that fashion. Although a closer look at the players' reasoning that produces these results is postponed till Chapter 8, we may enter a short discussion of the reasons for this effect of conservatism. One possible explanation may be stated in terms of minimising regret (Bell, 1982). Standing with 16 or less, when according to Basic one should hit, has actually two aspects: although it prevents the possibility of the player busting, this apparent advantage is offset by the fact that the player cannot win the hand unless the dealer goes bust. However, losing by busting may seem psychologically quite different from losing to a dealer's superior total. If the player hits and busts, only the player can be blamed for the outcome. In contrast, if the player stands but loses nevertheless, the blame can be transferred to the dealer or can be attributed to dealer's luck. Passing, so to speak, the control of the outcome to the dealer can thus minimise the possible regret, because the players believe that they can control their own decisions but obviously cannot control the dealer's drawing.

An alternative explanation, offered to us by Daniel Kahneman, is based on the common observation that people often tend to delay the receipt of bad news and maintain the illusory hope that reality will perhaps change in the course of time. Indeed, with a player's total between 12 and 16 the probability of losing is high, ranging between 0.60 and 0.85 even if Basic is perfectly followed. By deciding to stand early, players can defer the bad news to a later stage (namely to the point at which the dealer has to draw) while keeping the hope that the hand can still be won. The difference in winning probabilities between standing and hitting is the price paid for the luxury of deferring the bad news. Yates and Watts (1975) provide some empirical evidence that suggests preference for deferred losses.

A third interpretation can be put forward in terms of attentional bias. Because busting is an important and dramatic feature of the game, players may be totally occupied in evaluating probabilities of busting and pay little attention to the winning or losing probabilities when neither player nor dealer busts. Indeed, those situations in which players exhibit conservatism are characterised by relatively high probabilities of busting that supposedly dominate the player's attention.

The second finding is that players depart from the Basic strategy in an orderly way. The data in Fig. 2.2 reveal that, for each value of the dealer's card, the probability that a player hits is perfectly ranked (except for one minor reversal) with the player's total. As the players' totals increase they are more likely to stand, probably because of increasing fear of busting.The probability of busting is presented in Table 2.2, for players and dealers separately.

Indeed, player's total is perfectly correlated with player's probability of busting by hitting once. In a similar manner, there is, within each row, an orderly progression of the probability that a player hits (with only a few reversals), if the values of dealer's card 2-6 and 7-ace are treated separately. The ranking in this case is related to dealer's probability of busting; players are more likely to stand as that probability increases. Again, this ranking is highly correlated with dealer's probability of busting at the end of the round.

The results presented in Fig. 2.2 do not support the notion that players' behaviour is adequately described by the Basic rules. Basic is quite simple and could probably be learned within the hour. Still players with hundreds of hours experience do not follow it. But they learned to employ something better than level 1 strategies such as *never bust* or *mimic the dealer*.

The orderly structure of the data presented in Fig. 2.2 suggests a simple mathematical description of hitting behaviour, in which the probability of busting for player and dealer are the parameters:

$$P_{ij} = f(x_i, y_j)$$
(Form. 2.1)

in which i is player's total (i = 12, ...16); j = dealer's upcard (j = 2, ...10, ace); p_{ij} = the probability of hitting in each cell (i, j); x_i = the probability of the player busting as a function of total i; and y_j = the probability of the dealer busting as a function of upcard j. One problem with such a formula is that p_{ij} should be bounded between 0 and 1. A class of models which ensure that p_{ij} stays within these boundaries is called *logistic linear models*. A solution of our problem within this class could be:

$$\log\left(\frac{P_{ij}}{1 - P_{ij}}\right) = a \cdot x_i + b \cdot y_j + c$$
(Form. 2.2)

$\log\left(\dfrac{P_{ij}}{1 - P_{ij}}\right)$ runs from $-\infty$ to $+\infty$ when P_{ij} runs from 0 to 1

Since the values of x_i and y_j are the constants presented in Table 2.2, the only free parameters in the model are a, b, and c. Of these c only serves to adjust the grand mean; a and b represent the weights players attach to avoidance of busting, and to standing because they expect the dealer to bust.

The estimates of a, b, and c were obtained with the help of the GLIM computer program (Baker & Nelder, 1978), which applies the method of maximum likelihood to generalised linear models (Nelder & Wedderburn, 1972). The estimated parameters

TABLE 2.2
Probability of Busting for Players (After One Hit) and
Dealers (at the End of the Round, Possibly after
Several Hits)

i = Player's Total (Hard Hand Non-pair)	Prob. of Busting (x_i)	j= Dealer's Upcard	Prob. of Busting (y_j)
12	0.308	2	0.353
13	0.385	3	0.376
14	0.462	4	0.403
15	0.538	5	0.429
16	0.615	6	0.421
		7	0.260
		8	0.239
		9	0.233
		10	0.214
		Ace	0.116

are a = -15.1 and b = -13.7. GLIM described the goodness of fit by a chi-square, which is called deviance. In the present case the deviance was 136 which is significant with df = 47 at p< 0.001.

The reason for this deviance is that the relationship between dealer's probability of busting and the tendency to stand is not linear. For favourable upcards (7 to ace) players do not vary their hitting tendency very much, whereas they react more strongly to unfavourable upcards (2 to 6). This can be modelled by the addition of higher order terms describing the impact of yj:

$$\log \left(\frac{P_{ij}}{1 - P_{ij}} \right) = a \cdot x_i + b \cdot y_j + c \cdot y_j^2 + d \cdot y_j^3 + e \qquad \text{(Form. 2.3)}$$

The deviance of this model was 67, which with df = 45 is barely significant at p = 0.05.

In words formula 2.3 says that subjects follow a level 2 strategy. Their probability of hitting does not jump from nought to one, as prescribed by the Basic strategy, but varies continuously as a function of probability of busting for both player and dealer. The weight attached to a player's probability of busting is the same along the whole scale. The dealer's probability of busting receives more weight when it increases.

Conservative Doubling

The analysis so far has been restricted to hitting decisions for hard hands (totalling 12 to 17), but the conclusions are further supported by the data regarding doubling. The data on doubling consist of 1307 observations, with a range of 28 to 48 observations per cell, except for dealer's upcard 10 for which the range is 112 to 163. The player whose first two cards total 9, 10, or 11 may double down, that is, double the bet and then receive just one additional card. According to Basic, a player holding a total of 9 should double against a dealer's 3, 4, 5, or 6; holding a total of 10, the player should double except when dealer has a 10 or an ace; and with a total of 11, one should always double except against a dealer's ace. The conservatism phenomenon was again apparent from the doubling data. Players doubled on only 63.1% of the occasions when they were supposed to double (i.e., 36.9% violations of Basic), whereas they refused doubling on 79.5% of the occasions when Basic required such refusal (i.e., 20.5% violations of Basic). Thus players would rather incorrectly refuse doubling than double against the rules of Basic. The data on splitting (i.e., converting, for example, a pair of eights into two separate hands) were too few to be analysed, yet suggested a similar pattern.

Insurance Decisions

Whenever the dealer's upcard is an ace, the player may opt to insure. A player who insures places an additional side bet not greater than half the original bet. If the dealer indeed obtains a blackjack the player wins twice the amount of insurance; otherwise, the bet is lost. Suppose that the player places b units as insurance. The dealer's probability of obtaining a blackjack given that the first upcard is an ace is approximately 4/13, because 4 out of the 13 different cards in a suit have a value of 10. Hence, the player has a probability of 4/13 of winning 2b units and a probability of 9/13 of losing b (the insurance premium). This yields a negative expected value of approximately -7.7% of the amount of insurance placed. Players should never insure unless they are counters, in which case they should insure when the relative number of 10s left in the shoe is large enough to yield a positive expected value.

Nevertheless, the majority of the players in our sample did insure, at least on some occasions. Of the 112 players, 14 (12.5%) insured whenever possible, 53 (47.5%) used the option occasionally, and 44 (40%) never insured (one player with a small number of hands never encountered an insurance opportunity during the observation period).

Why do players insure when the expected value of such an action is negative? Insurance is a separate gamble on whether or not the dealer's second card will be a 10-value card. The probability of this event is a function of the proportion of 10-value cards remaining in the shoe and is thus virtually independent of the player's current total. We propose that the very label of this special bet, *insurance*, suggests that the gamble is in some way related to the original gamble; in particular it is seen as related to the player's two-card total. The power of the label *insurance* has been shown by Slovic, Fischhoff, and Lichtenstein (1982) in a slightly different gambling situation. There, a sure loss was more often preferred to the probability of a larger loss when the sure loss was called *insurance*.

In order to obtain further insight into the pattern of insurance decisions, we limited the analysis to the sub-sample of players who insured occasionally. Table 2.3 presents

TABLE 2.3
Percentage of Times in
Which Players Use the
Insurance Option as a
Function of Player's
Total

Player's Total	Insurance Percentage
4-10	28
11	38
12	53
13	36
14	41
15	46
16	53
17	35
18	26
19	42
20	72

the percentage of times that players used the insurance option as a function of player's total. By far the highest percentage of insurance occurs when the player's total is 20. Because 20 is a very attractive hand, many players do not want to lose this valuable asset and consequently insure it. This interpretation has been substantiated by interviews with a large number of players (see Chapter 8 for more details), many of whom explicitly said that they insure only a good hand. This may be another instance of avoiding regret. Other players, however, said that they also insure really bad hands such as 12 or 16 points. Sixteen is unfavourable because of the high probability of busting when drawing another card. Having 12 is considered bad because if the players had only one or two points less, they would have a favourable total of 11 or 10. Examination of Table 2.3 shows that players often follow the strategy of insuring totals of 12, 16, or 20 points, which from a normative viewpoint should be considered as throwing good money after bad.

Players' Consistency

Formula 2.3 describes the behaviour of players by means of probabilities. That is, for each combination of players' total and dealer's up card it described the probability that a player will hit. Nothing is said about what, in the end, makes a player decide to hit. The probability only represents an overall tendency to let the decision go one way or the other, but it is not reasonable to assume that players flip some sort of mental coin in order to reach a decision. The discussion of the reasoning that guides players in these situations is postponed to Chapter 8. At present we will only discuss one possible factor that could have produced our results.

This originates from the fact that the results presented in Fig. 2.2 are accumulated over subjects. The probability of hitting in a cell could reflect probabilistic behaviour in all individuals but also all-or-none behaviour. In the latter case some subjects would always stand, while others would always hit. The cell entries in Fig. 2.2 represent, in that case, only the percentages of subjects that hit or stand. Formula 2.3 would describe the group results but possibly not the behaviour of any individual player. Unfortunately it is practically impossible to collect sufficient data about individual players, such that the model could be tested on individual data. However, a closer look at the consistency of individual players can give some indication. If formula 2.3 described the behaviour of individual players we should find a fair degree of inconsistency within players.

In order to determine the extent to which players' decisions were consistent, the individual data were analysed separately. This analysis focussed on those cases in which the player was confronted more than once with the same situation (i.e., the same combination of player's total and dealer's upcard). From the sample of 112 players only 16 (approximately 14%) exhibited a perfectly consistent decision pattern in such situations. This figure is probably an over-estimation because those players for whom we had a relatively small number of observations had few repeated cases and hence had little opportunity to display inconsistency. To obtain a more reliable estimate, all the players who had fewer than six cells with at least two repetitions were eliminated from the sample. From the 88 players left, only 4 (approximately 5%) were perfectly consistent, and the majority of the remainder exhibited several inconsistent decisions. This still does not prove that the probabilistic model applies to individual players, but it renders the all-or-none model less likely.

Betting Patterns

The rules of blackjack require that all bets (except insurance) are placed before any cards are dealt. From a normative viewpoint, only counting methods prescribe how to vary bets in a systematic way. Yet, our observations suggest that the majority of players use betting patterns that cannot be justified on normative grounds. What is the nature of these betting strategies?

In Chapter 4 we will analyse some betting patterns used by system players in roulette, such as the Martingale system and the d'Alembert system. The idea behind these systems is to increase the bet after a loss, so that previous losses are compensated by future wins. The snag in all these systems is that the casinos impose a maximum bet and that players' capital is limited. Still, the employment of such a system requires careful planning and dogged application of strict rules, which should be immediately discernible from betting patterns. Other players might have the objective of stretching their play as long as possible. Usually that entails not increasing or even lowering the bets during a period of losses. Thus something about a player's objectives is revealed by a closer study of betting patterns.

We analysed the betting behaviour of 55 individual players in our sample, each of whom played at least 75 hands. The hands of each player were categorised in a 2 x 3 table according to whether the previous hand was lost or won, and whether the bet was increased, decreased or unaltered, relative to the previous hand.

Ties between the dealer's total and that of the players were classified as follows: most players perceive a tie of 20, 21, or blackjack as a loss, because with such a valuable hand they have high expectations of winning. A tie under those circumstances can yield disappointment and a feeling of bad luck. On the other hand, tying with a total of 17, 18, or 19 is often considered by players as an achievement because they were able to avoid a loss. Hence, all ties with a total of 20, 21, or blackjack were categorised as losses, and all ties with a total of 17, 18, or 19 were categorised as wins. Eight players who changed the size of their bets less than 20% of the time were omitted from further analysis because their numbers of observations in the four remaining cells were not sufficient for a chi-square test.

Each table corresponding to the 47 players remaining in the sample was subjected to a separate 2 x 3 chi-square analysis. Using a p value of 0.10 as a criterion, we found 27 players with a significant interaction between bet size and outcome of the previous round. With a criterion of $p = 0.10$ one would, under the null hypothesis, expect to find approximately five players reaching significance. The finding of 27 players obtaining a p value less than 0.10 is significant at $p < 0.001$. Thus, out of 55 players only 27, which is 49%, changed their bets as a function of previous outcome. Of these 27 players, three showed no clear pattern in the variation of their bets. Decrease and increase of bets was not related to losing or winning in a simple manner. The rest of the players could be classified into two groups, using different strategies. Eleven players usually varied their bet by increasing it after a lost hand and decreasing it after a hand that was won. Thirteen players varied their bet in the opposite direction: they tended to increase their bets after winning and decrease their bets after losing. Personal interviews, discussed in Chapter 8, revealed that this second group of players base their strategy on a belief in periods of good and bad luck. If one is winning, one should increase one's bets in order to use the period of good luck. When one is losing, bets should be decreased to a minimum, because one might experience a period of bad luck. The plausibility of these explanations will be further discussed in Chapters 7 and 8.

Net Result

The net result per player, expressed by the average percentage won or lost, is presented in Fig. 2.3.

On the basis of the study with 574 players we may expect an overall loss percentage of 2.9%. This grand mean, and the 95% confidence interval around this mean

$$\pm 1.96/\sqrt{N} \ (N = \text{number of hands played})$$

are also sketched in Fig. 2.3. It is obvious that the large majority of players fall within the interval. On the basis of statistical fluctuations 2.5% of 112, or three players, are expected to do worse, and the same number to do better. The actual result corresponds

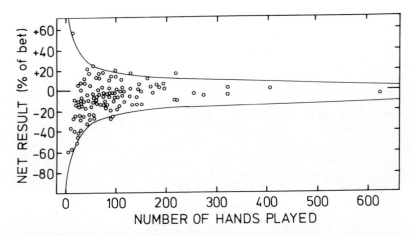

FIG. 2.3   Net results of 112 blackjack players in an Amsterdam casino.

closely with this expectation. This confirms the notion that the group means presented before are representative of individual players, and that the differences among their outcomes are mostly a matter of statistical fluctuation.

CONCLUSION

This chapter is subtitled "the game players refuse to win." Blackjack is the only casino game in which the player's strategy influences the net expected result. Strategies of increasing difficulty level promise increasing pay offs. What we have seen in this chapter is that players do not refuse to learn. The strategy characterised by formula 2.3 is the result of acquiring 15 probabilities, at least on rank order level. But players rarely acquire the optimal strategy, although this strategy is widely publicised and not difficult to learn. Are players not really interested in winning, even when they play 25 hours a week, and spend very large sums of money?

CHAPTER 3

Objectives of Blackjack Players

An interesting aspect of the game of blackjack is that it offers many choices, and that the outcome depends on how these choices are made. The players can achieve different goals or objectives. This chapter discusses an empirical study of what these objectives might be.

One objective that springs to mind immediately is maximisation of expected value. The results presented in the previous chapter suggest that the vast majority of players do not try to achieve this objective. Maximisation of expected value is obtained by card counters only; in our sample of 112 players not one card counter was identified. The objective could be toned down a little if we adopt some limiting but reasonable marginal conditions, perhaps derived from some notion of bounded rationality (Simon, 1957). Counting requires the acquisition of a formal set of rules, a training period of several months, a large capital and a continuous investment of playing time. It is not reasonable to expect that occasional casino visitors would go to such lengths, simply because they do not plan to play a sufficient number of hours.

For habitual players the story is different. In the study of 77 experienced players which will be reported in this chapter, we found that the median frequency of visits to casinos was two nights a week; 22 players gambled four or more nights a week. The casinos in which this study was made, offered an average of 40 rounds an hour, and players stay at the tables for an average of six hours. The median gambler in our sample could therefore be expected to play about 24,000 hands a year. In Chapter 2 we have already calculated that the application of counting methods in 24,000 hands promises a 99% chance of finishing with a positive result. The amount that can be won depends on the size of the bets placed when the count is favourable. In the Dutch casinos the maximum bet is usually Dfl. 500. Favourable situations occur in about 15% of rounds (cf. Keren, Wagenaar & Krul, 1982), or six times an hour. This implies that the bets placed in an hour total Dfl. 3000. Perfect counting and favourable casino rules ensure an average profit of 1.5%, or Dfl. 45 ($22) an hour, or Dfl. 27,000 ($13,000) a year. This amount should be worth the investment of energy and time, and one should wonder why only two of these players ever considered card counting. One step down from card counting is the Basic strategy, which can be learned with not more than one hour of study and probably a few hours of practice. It requires the insight of the existence of an optimal strategy, and the knowledge that this strategy is known and made available in published books. It also requires the willingness to play according to strict rules. A Basic player does not really play, but behaves like a little computer. The thrill stems from the uncertainty about winning or losing, not from the challenge of making the correct decisions. A Basic player, playing two nights a week and betting an average of Dfl. 25 should expect to lose Dfl. 5 an hour, or Dfl. 3000 a year, which is not unreasonable for any type of amusement. The difference when compared with the modal strategy displayed by the 112 casino players described in the previous chapter is considerable: with the same assumptions they would lose Dfl. 27 an hour, or Dfl. 16,200 ($8500) a year. Apart from the fact that such a hobby is quite expensive, we should wonder why the difference of about Dfl. 13,000 ($6000) does not motivate people to learn how to play Basic. Even with the assumption that card counting is a too complex strategy for the majority of players, it is difficult to believe that maximisation of monetary profit is the motivating factor at the blackjack table. A supporting argument is the fact that the large numbers of hands played by the players in the group of 77, discussed in this chapter, allows little deviation from the mean expected loss. The standard deviation after 24,000 hands is 0.64%. The probability of overcoming the negative odds of 2.7% is about 1 in 1000. This means that players, who play two nights a week, employing strategies as described in the previous chapter, *must* experience a loss after one year. It is simply not feasible that they lack a motivation to learn Basic, just because they are winning anyway.

The question addressed in this chapter is simple. What do gamblers expect to achieve in the casino? The almost instinctive answer, "to maximize their winnings," is obviously not correct. One of the alternative answers is that people violate axiom 5 discussed in Chapter 1, which implies that taking a risk has a utility of itself. It is not unreasonable that gamblers gamble instead of going to theatres or sports events, just because they enjoy running risks, and are willing to pay the price. Still other answers are related to the very complex reasonings that may accompany gambling behaviour. It is, for instance, possible that players discount previous losses, assuming that they can in some miraculous way be compensated by future winnings. In conclusion, the reason for studying players' objectives is that we want to answer two closely related questions:

1) Why do players use inferior strategies? In particular, why do they fail to acquire Basic either by learning from experience, or by buying one of the many simple guides?

2) Why do players continue to visit casinos, and play a game in which they lose?

Obviously gamblers dislike losing and like to win. But winning cannot be their only objective. Gambling must have other utilities. What are the other attributes in a multi-attribute utility structure of gambling?

AN EXPERIMENT WITH 77 HABITUAL GAMBLERS

Parts of this study were reported before by Wagenaar, Keren and Pleit-Kuiper (1984). The dimensions of perceived utility of playing blackjack were investigated by asking players to express a degree to which they concur with 45 statements about blackjack. Examples of such statements are:

(1)   If in another casino blackjack paid three times instead of one-and-a-half, I would always go there.

(45)   After four low cards a 10 is almost certain to appear.

A complete list of the 45 statements is presented in Tables 3.1 to 3.3. The selection of statements was based on an extensive pilot study comprising 33 players. Since the results in this pilot were essentially the same as the results presented here, they will not be discussed further. The statements were printed on 10 x 14 cm cards in double-sized typewriter letters. Both Dutch and English versions of the statements were used since seven players understood only English. Casino gambling is an international affair.

The players indicated their degree of agreement by sorting the cards into three piles which were labelled agree, indifferent, and disagree. Then each pile was sorted in two parts on the basis of stronger of lesser agreement or disagreement. Thus each statement received an agreement rating on a six point scale. There was no predetermined upper or lower limit to the number of cards placed in each pile.

The subjects were 77 experienced blackjack players visiting two of the government-owned casinos in The Netherlands. In these casinos six-deck shoes are used. The players were invited to participate in the experiment by employees of the casino. The employees selected players they knew by sight, through frequent visits. The interviews took place in a quiet corner of the casino restaurant and lasted an average of 20 minutes. Players were only excluded when they appeared not to understand either Dutch or English. Thirty-four players were female, 43 male. The median reported frequency of visits to casinos was two nights a week; 22 gambled four or more nights a week. After completion of the experiment players were rewarded with a free drink.

A list of statements that players agreed with on the whole is presented in Table 3.1. The two first statements (7, 5) offer options which are attractive and which are easily understood by players, because they do, in fact, eliminate two rules that cause a lot of frustration: after splitting of aces the player receives only one additional card on each hand; if the second card is a 10-value card the entire hand does not count as a blackjack.

The third statement (43) reflects a belief that is hard to reconcile with a rational consideration of the game. The seven players sitting at a blackjack table each play their

TABLE 3.1
Statements With Which Players Did on the Whole Agree[a]

		Rating	
No.	Statement	Mean	S.D.
7.	It is better for the player if you can receive more than one card after splitting aces.	1.51	1.11
5.	I would like it if ace-ten also counted as blackjack after splitting.	1.57	1.30
43.	A bad player can spoil the game for everyone.	1.61	1.22
26.	It is not so bad to lose Dfl. 20.	1.75	1.35
31.	You only know whether your decisions were correct after the round is over.	1.96	1.55
40.	It is good that the casino has a dress code.	2.01	1.60
16.	If you are very unlucky on a particular day you should quit playing.	2.25	1.75
6.	When I lose with 20 points I feel worse than when I lose with 13 points.	2.28	1.79
28.	A bad player often asks for too many cards.	2.33	1.92
38.	When you play on two boxes you may protect one with the other.	2.35	1.78
4.	It would be better if doubling was allowed with more than two cards.	2.45	1.83

[a]Score 1.0 to 2.50; numbers in the first column reflect order of presentation.

individual game, against the dealer. It is not clear what a "bad" player is (but see statement no. 28), but it is even more amazing that a bad player could affect the chances of other players. Only through prolonged interviews could we obtain an explanation of this belief. These interviews will be discussed in Chapter 8. At present we will only accept the suggestion that players think of blackjack as a team sport, in which seven players try to beat the house in a co-operative effort.

The fifth statement on the list (no. 31) is directly relevant to the question of whether players apply fixed strategies. Within a fixed strategy like *mimic the dealer*, Basic, or a counting method, decisions are determined by parameters of the decision situation, such as player's total, dealer's upcard, or deck composition. A decision is correct if it is in accordance with the rule. Correct decisions lead to optimal outcomes in the long run, not in every instance. Hence the immediate outcome is not an appropriate basis for the determination of decision quality. The general agreement with statement 31 signifies that subjects do not have good understanding of the long-run principle, and probably also that they do not apply fixed rules. The distinction between fixed strategies adopted on the basis of long-term considerations and ever-changing reasoning that is influenced by a multitude of arbitrarily selected and passing arguments, runs parallel with the distinction between *aleatory* and *epistemic* reasoning (cf. Beach, Barnes, & Christensen-Szalanski, 1986) which will be further discussed in Chapter 8.

The preference for a dress code (tie and jacket for men) is somewhat surprising.

Apparently the "classy" atmosphere of the casino is an important attribute. One player said: "I don't mind losing a thousand guilders, but I want to lose it in style."

Statement no. 16 represents in another way the belief already expressed in no. 43, viz. that subsequent hands are mutually dependent. By continuous losing you can discover that you are not lucky. Players believe that losing hands should be followed by winning hands, in accordance with the well-known gamblers' fallacy. If this does not happen, players feel that they are experiencing bad luck (see Chapter 7). Some intuitive understanding is provided by statement 6: when I lose with 20 points in my hand I feel worse than when I lose with 13 points. The losses incurred by the two events and the effects on the long-term result are the same. The regret is much more acute in the first case, because the player was quite certain to win. But apart from the regret, repeatedly losing against all odds creates the need for an explanation. If there is a hidden factor, causing unexpected losses, it would be better to stop. The question is: how many unexpected losses are needed to create the suggestion that there is such a hidden cause, called bad luck? We will discuss this further in Chapter 7. But obviously, players assume that something, like "bad luck," can be detected and that it may last for a considerable time.

The response to statement 28 is in full agreement with the conservative decisions observed in Chapter 2. In general players tend to stand when they should hit, rather than making the opposite error. In the same way they fail to double or to split. A bad player, who may spoil the game of the others, is apparently not conforming to this conservatism. Basic players and card counters are called bad players by most of the others, which in turn demonstrates that most players do not apply these strategies.

Statement no.38 presents another demonstration of the assumed dependence between hands. Players may take two adjacent boxes and place bets on both. The idea is that losing one hand can be compensated by winning the other. From a normative viewpoint playing a losing strategy in two boxes just doubles the speed of losing.

The list of statements to which players are on the whole indifferent is presented in Table 3.2. The agreement within the group is virtually constant across these questions: the standard deviation is always close to two points. The large majority of these statements were included to facilitate the principal components analysis presented in a later section. Still, some of the statements deserve some discussion here.

Statement no.20 is related to an extremely sensitive issue among gamblers: the task of the player on the seventh box. Cards not taken by this player go to the dealer. Hence the seventh-box player controls the dealer's result. The problem is, of course, that the seventh-box player does not know what the next card will be. Still at blackjack tables there are many discussions about what the player at the seventh box should do, or should have done. At many tables the other players request that the seventh- box players sacrifice themselves by ruining their own hands, with the purpose of ruining the dealer's hands as well. Again, there is no way in which a non-counting seventh-box player could achieve this goal. In our sample, experienced players do not wholeheartedly agree with this opinion, but they do not reject it either.

Statement no.15 reflects the notion of "playing on the house." The idea is that a

TABLE 3.2

Statements to Which Players on the Whole Were Indifferent[a]

		Rating	
No.	Statement	Mean	S.D.
21.	I like doubling and splitting because it makes the game more exciting.	2.52	1.93
19.	It is not so bad to lose Dfl. 100.	2.56	1.75
8.	I prefer blackjack to roulette because with blackjack you have greater control of the game.	2.60	1.77
13.	It would be fun if you received a bottle of champagne with three sevens.	2.64	1.80
24.	It is wise to increase your bet if you are winning.	2.70	1.71
20.	Players on the seventh box should occasionally sacrifice themselves for the benefit of the other players.	2.70	2.02
15.	I only bet very high when I have made a profit.	2.71	2.00
10.	Before playing, I always set a maximum that I am willing to lose.	2.75	2.01
36.	You should not start betting too high because then the game may be over too soon.	2.79	1.93
1.	If in another casino blackjack paid three times instead of one-and-a-half I would always go there.	2.82	2.05
2.	The casino ought to return 10% of your loss.	2.91	1.99
14.	To become a good blackjack player you should play several nights a week.	3.13	1.98
34.	You should only insure a good hand.	3.17	1.99
37.	The entertainment of the game is more important than winning.	3.31	1.92
22.	Doubling is more important than splitting.	3.39	1.80
35.	You should not double as often when you are losing.	3.43	2.00
30.	You should avoid playing against extremely lucky dealers.	3.62	1.97
45.	After four low cards a ten is almost certain to appear.	3.62	1.80
32.	Go to the casino with friends and not alone.	3.88	1.72
25.	It is better if only the seven players at the table are allowed to bet.	4.04	2.11
29.	You lose a higher bet more often than a lower one.	4.05	1.77
23.	It is wise to increase your bet after you have lost.	4.25	1.72
3.	It would be better if the maximum bet per box was Dfl. 2500.	4.35	1.93
12.	Two decks in the shoe is better than six.	4.45	1.82

[a]Score 2.51 to 4.50.

profit consists of money that does not really belong to you. With money that in fact belongs to "the house" you can take greater risks, because the worst that could happen is that the house gets its own money back. This reasoning leads us to the question of adjustment of the *status quo* to previous losses or profits, which will be taken up again in Chapter 8. Players do not reject the connection between bet size and profit, and in principle it is not illogical to become less risk averse when wealth increases. But it is necessary to view the results of an evening as if it was a separate entity, not related to the large losses incurred during previous visits.

The unenthusiastic reaction to statement no. 1 came as a big surprise. Players can expect to receive a blackjack in 4.7% of the hands. Doubling of their reward would get them an extra 7.1% which would turn their expected loss of 2.7% into a profit of 4.4%. Players have little intuitive understanding of this quantitative aspect of the game, or they have suspected that the advantage would be compensated for by some hidden extra costs.

In the same manner the reaction to statement 12 is illuminating. Players disagreed slightly with the idea of having only two decks in a shoe. The reason is that the game would be stopped frequently for shuffling, which is disliked. (See also statement no. 41 in Table 3.3.) On the other hand, uneven shoe compositions which are favourable for card counters, occur more frequently when there are only a few decks in a shoe. The profits of counters playing a system described by Keren, Wagenaar and Krul (1982) decrease from 4.0 to 1.0% when the number of decks increased from four to

TABLE 3.3
Statements with Which Players Did on the Whole Disagree[a]

No.	Statement	Rating	
		Mean	S.D.
11.	It would be better if the minimum bet per box was Dfl. 1.	4.78	1.77
18.	It is not so bad to lose Dfl. 500.	4.97	1.83
33.	Eight decks in the shoe is better than six.	4.97	1.31
17.	It would be better if a machine would do a fast shuffle after every round.	5.00	1.53
9.	It would be more fun to play with real money instead of chips.	5.01	1.73
39.	It would be better if the maximum bet per box was Dfl. 100.	5.05	1.40
42.	Splitting cards should not be allowed.	5.10	1.63
27.	It would be better if the minimum bet per box was Dfl. 25.	5.25	1.45
44.	It would be better if doubling was not allowed after splitting.	5.25	1.10
41.	It would be better if the dealer shuffled after each round.	5.49	1.14

[a]Score 4.51 to 6.00.

eight. Habitual casino visitors apparently do not attach much importance to this aspect of the game. The reason is, of course, that they do not count.

A list of statements with which habitual players disagreed is presented in Table 3.3. Some of the disagreements are quite remarkable. Players do not want to have the option of betting small amounts like one guilder. The table minima in the casino were Dfl. 5 and Dfl. 10. The reason why one would object to a decrease is that this would allow a number of "amateur old ladies" to influence the outcome of the game. This again reveals the belief that winning or losing in blackjack depends on the behaviour of the other players at the table. As one player remarked: "I do not want to lose Dfl. 500, when an old lady betting one guilder takes the wrong decision."

The reaction to statement 17 throws some light on the origin of some of the responses. In statement 12 they objected to decreasing the number of decks in a shoe. Now they also object to an increase. Apparently the current number of six decks in the shoe is exactly right. There is, on mathematical grounds, no reason to prefer six decks, but, as one player expressed: "If the casino changes it, they do it to increase their profit; let us leave it the way it is now." It is possible that many responses were inspired by this type of reasoned conservatism.

Principal Components Analysis of Responses

The scores were analysed by the Princals program (De Leeuw & Van Rijckevorsel, 1979). This program performs an analysis of principal components which assumes that the raw data are on an ordinal or interval scale. Princals defines orthogonal dimensions which do not allow rotation. The stimuli (statements) are presented as points in the space defined by these dimensions, whereas the players are presented as vectors on which the stimulus points are projected, thus yielding an ordering of the stimuli which by numerical iteration is made to parallel the expressed degree of agreement as well as possible.

The analysis yielded three interpretable dimensions, accounting for about half of the total variance. The normalised eigen-values were 0.366, 0.056 and 0.047 in the numerical solution, and 0.409, 0.041 and 0.056 in the ordinal solution. In the ordinal solution only the rank order relations among the ratings are interpreted, in the numerical solution the ratings are assumed to lie on an interval scale.

Since the differences between the ordinal and the numerical solution were negligible only the numerical solution will be presented. The reader should keep in mind that the significance of dimensions should not be judged solely on the basis of eigen-values, but also by asking whether the rank ordering of statements along these dimensions can be meaningfully interpreted. The reason is that eigen-values are fully determined by the initial selection of stimuli. The reader should also realise that labelling, as in any factor-analytical approach, is quite arbitrary. Rather the labels should be used as aids, which assist in interpreting the uncovered structure.

The three-dimensional solutions are presented in Figs. 3.1 to 3.4. The interpretation of these figures is as follows.

Dimension 1: Expected Value.   On the first dimension the statements are ordered such that considerations of expected value are reflected. Statements suggesting that the expected value should increase are on the right. For instance:

(5) I would like it if ace-ten also counted as blackjack after splitting.

(7) It is better for the player if you can receive more than one card after splitting aces.

On the left side we find statements that imply decrease in expected value, as for example:

(27) It would be better if the minimum bet per box was Dfl. 25.

(41) It would be better if the dealer shuffled after each round.

(44) It would be better if doubling was not allowed after splitting.

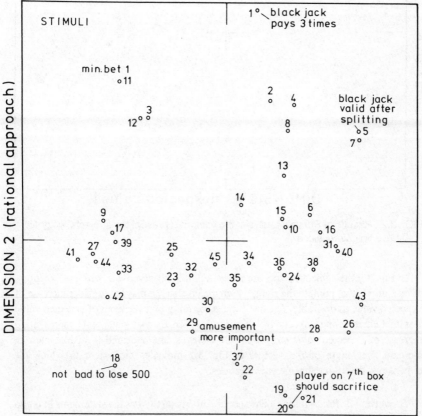

FIG. 3.1 Results of Princals analysis: the position of statements in the plane defined by the two first dimensions.

MICHAEL FRANK
PSYCHOLOGY DEPT.

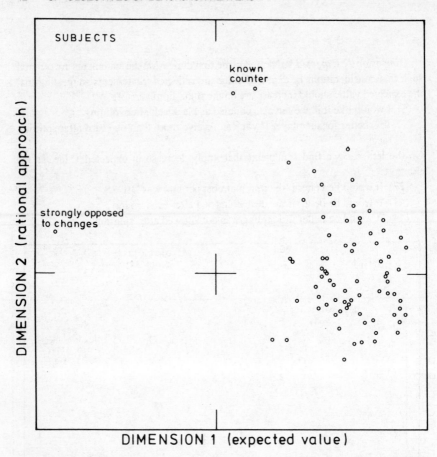

FIG. 3.2   Results of Princals analysis: the vectors represent the subjects' weightings of the two first dimensions.

In Fig. 3.2 the subject vectors are presented. It is observed that with the exception of one, all vectors point to the right, which means that the players consider increase of expected value as desirable. The one subject rejecting improvement of expected value was in fact rejecting any change of the rules. Since most statements representing increase of expected value suggested rule changes, she appeared to dislike such an increase.The length of the vectors in Fig. 3.2 indicates the extent to which the dimensions determine the agreement ratings.

Dimension 2: Rationality.   The second dimension divides the statements into two groups (Fig. 3.3). The statements to the right are endorsed by players who feel that an increase in the number of options allows the players to utilise their skills better, that winning depends on the utilisation of skills, and that the objective of gambling is to win. To the left you find statements reflecting the opinion that luck and all sorts of unchecked beliefs are more important than your own reasoning, and that the major objective of gambling is amusement and the experience of excitement. For the sake of simplicity we will label these two extremes of the scale "rational" and "non-rational," without the intention of introducing the connotation of a smart-stupid distinction. Examples of the "rational" attitude are:

(11) It would be better if the minimum bet per box was Dfl. 1.

(8) I prefer blackjack to roulette because with blackjack you have greater control of the game.

(1) If, in another casino, blackjack paid three times instead of one-and-a-half I would always go there.

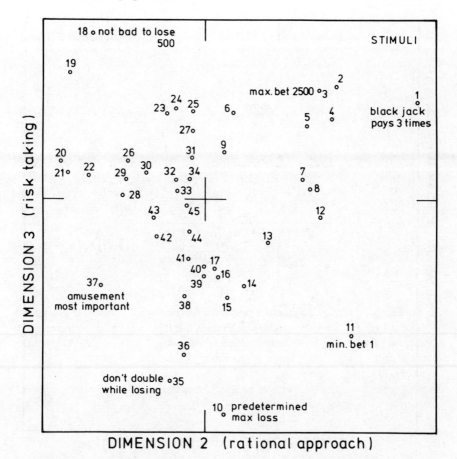

FIG. 3.3 Results of Princals analysis: the positions of statements in the plane defined by the second and third dimensions.

Examples of the "non-rational" attitude are:
(20) Players on the seventh box should occasionally sacrifice themselves for the benefit of the other players.
(21) I like doubling and splitting because it makes the game more exciting.
(37) The entertainment of the game is more important than winning.

The players disagreed considerably about the valuation of this dimension (Fig. 3.4); 36 have vectors to the right and 41 have vectors to the left. Among the extremes we find one known card counter who shares the conception of blackjack as an intellectual challenge and abhors the statements resting on false intuitions.

Dimension 3: Risk Attitude.   The ordering of statements along the third dimension

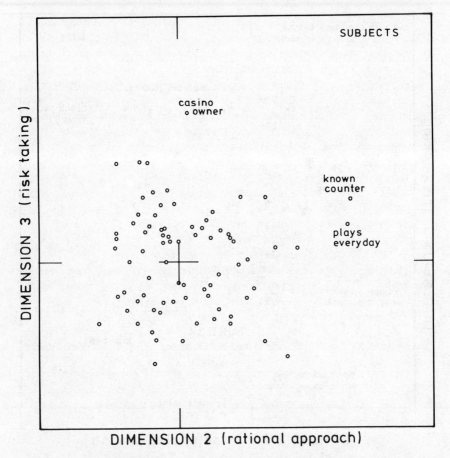

FIG.   3.4   Results of Princals analysis: the vectors represent the subjects' weightings of the second and third dimension.

seems to reflect risk attitudes. High on this dimension are statements like:

(3) It would be better if the maximum bet per box was Dfl. 2500.

(18) It is not so bad to lose Dfl. 500.

Low on this dimension we find:

(10) Before playing I always set a maximum that I am willing to lose.

(11) It would be better if the minimum bet per box was Dfl. 1.

(35) You should not double as often when you are losing.

(36) You should not start betting too high because then the game may be over too soon.

Again the players do not agree on the desirability of risk: 43 players are on the side of risk seeking, 34 on the side of risk aversion. The extreme risk taker was an owner of illegal casinos who spends his leisure time gambling (and losing) in state-owned casinos. I saw this man lose near to a million guilders in less than half an hour, and enjoying it! Another possible interpretation of dimension 3 is that it reflects the assets of the players; however, since assets were not known to the experimenters, there is little evidence to support such an interpretation.

The extent of the differences among players ordered in different quadrants of Fig. 3.3 can best be illustrated by looking at their reactions to some of the typical statements, as presented in Table 3.4. Examination of the columns of this table illustrates that players agree most with a statement when they are located in the same quadrant as that statement (the underlined scores) and that the differences within columns are considerable.

The statements are:

(1) If, in another casino, blackjack paid three times instead of one-and-a-half, I would always go there.

(11) It would be better, if the minimum bet per box was Dfl. 1

(19) It is not so bad to lose Dfl. 100.

(35) You should not double as often when you are losing.

The attributes of playing blackjack that besides expected value determine the utility of playing are ordered along two dimensions. One represents a frame concerning the

TABLE 3.4

Mean Responses of Subjects in the Four Quadrants of Fig. 3.3 to some Typical Statements[a]

Quadrant in which subjects are located	Mean response to statement no.			
	1	11	19	35
Rational				
Risk seeking	1.32	4.63	3.37	4.53
Risk averse	2.50	3.19	3.63	2.63
Non-rational				
Risk seeking	3.16	5.76	1.52	3.68
Risk averse	4.29	5.12	2.47	2.24

[a]1=complete agreement, 6=complete disagreement.

perceived nature and objective of the game; the other represents risk attitudes. Despite the high agreement among players concerning the role of expected value, they have very different opinions concerning the other dimensions. Dimensions 2 and 3 account only for a small proportion of the variance, but this does not mean that they are relatively unimportant for the determination of players' opinions. Statements like the ones presented in Table 3.4 are evidently endorsed or rejected on the basis of players' location along these dimensions, and it should not be at all difficult to formulate a multitude of similar extreme opinions. Thus dimensions 2 and 3 could be sufficiently important to counteract the preference for a positive expected value revealed by the first dimension.

CONCLUSION

Most players like to win. On the whole they endorse statements that imply an increase of expected value. The acceptance of games with a negative expected outcome cannot be explained by indifference with respect to winning, or worse, a fondness for losing. However, a preference for winning does not necessarily entail the mathematical normative concept and the narrow optimal strategy that follows from it. Many sub-optimal strategies have the aim of increasing winning probability, although they stem from a large variety of beliefs strongly anchored in an almost folkloristic perspective shared by many players, and not supported by mathematical theory. In a similar fashion the acceptance or avoidance of risk are both combined with a preference to winning. All players, risk seekers and risk avoiders, like to win; only they try to achieve this goal through different risk attitudes.

In conclusion then, it can be said that the irrational beliefs presented in this chapter, and the deviations from the optimal strategy demonstrated in the previous one, should not easily be interpreted as meaning that players are not interested in winning. They probably are. But a complicated structure of false or incomplete knowledge, and irrational beliefs, prevents them from achieving this goal.

CHAPTER 4

Roulette: The Game Players Should Not Hope to Win

Roulette is one of the oldest casino games. Invented or constructed by Blaise Pascal in the 17th century, it has become the classical example of a gambling device. The most common version has the numbers zero to 37, placed in a standardised order on a revolving disc. The rotary movement is controlled by the "balleur," and kept more or less constant. The ball is pressed against the rim of the bowl and launched when the number that came out in the previous round passes. The ball and the disc rotate in opposite directions. After several full rotations the ball leaves the rim, hits one of the spoilers, changes its direction and falls in one of the 37 pockets of the spinning wheel. This set up is designed to generate numbers in a random fashion. In a later chapter we will discuss whether a roulette wheel is indeed a perfect randomiser. First we will just assume that in every round every number has the same probability of occurrence, i.e. 1/37.

The essence of roulette is that players bet against the house on the number that will come out next. They can bet on single numbers (straight bet) or on combinations. Well-known combinations are two adjacent numbers (split bet), three numbers in a row (street bet), or a block of four numbers (square bet). Other combinations contain 6, 12 or 18 numbers. The payment rule is defined by :

$$V = \left(\frac{36}{n} - 1\right) \cdot b \qquad \text{(Form. 4.1)}$$

in which V is the payment; n represents on how many numbers the winning bet was placed; and b is the size of the winning bet. Thus, if a bet of Dfl. 100 is placed on the

47

square 23, 24, 26, 27, and 27 is the winning number, then the gain is Dfl. 800. The initial bet is also returned.

From formula 4.1 we can derive that the expected value for any bet equals:

$$EV = \frac{n}{37}\left(\frac{36}{n} - 1\right) b - \left(\frac{37 - n}{37}\right) b = -\frac{1}{37}b \qquad \text{(Form. 4.2)}$$

Thus expected value is minus 1/37th of the initial bet, irrespective of how the bet is placed. Provided that all numbers are equiprobable there is no number or number combination that could lead to an expected value better or worse than -1/37 b. The only exception to this rule is betting on the "simple chances" black and red, even and odd, low and high. When zero appears the bet is neither lost nor won, but placed "in prison." In the next round it can still be lost, or, when the right number comes out, be freed. When the bet is freed it can be removed from the table, but the bank does not pay a profit on top of it. In some casinos one is allowed to take back half of the bet instead of leaving it "in prison." In both cases the expected value of the even chances is -1/74 b Although the expected value for simple chances is twice as good as for the number combinations (the "multiple" chances), few players in practice prefer the simple chances. Therefore expected value cannot be the only criterion for placing bets. The interesting question is why gamblers are playing the numbers, and how they select a strategy.

SYSTEM PLAYING

Many people believe that the negative odds of roulette can be overcome through the application of a system. The best known ones are the Small and Big Martingale systems. The idea is that a player bets only on the simple chances. Bets are increased after losing, so that previous losses are made good. In the Small Martingale system, bet size increases thus:1, 2, 4, 8, 16, etc. After losing three rounds, 7 times (i.e. 1+2+4) the original bet has been lost. The new bet size of 8 makes up for these losses, and adds a profit of one unit. When a sequence of losses is ended by a win, one returns to the original bet size. The Big Martingale system adds a profit of one unit for each round played: 1, 3, 7, 15, 31, etc. After losing three rounds, 11 times (i.e. 1+3+7) the original bet has been lost. The new bet size of 15 makes up for these losses, and adds four units because altogether four rounds have been played.

The principle of the Martingale systems is that no loss is definitive. If the next bet is large enough, one can conclude each sequence with a profit, provided that the sequences are finished with a winning round before the table maximum is reached, and before one runs out of money. These mishaps occur usually only after a sequence of 10 or more losses. Some players try to prevent such losing sequences from occurring by following a predetermined order, such as: red-black-black-black-red-red-red-black-black-red, repeated endlessly. Using the Martingale system they can only lose if the roulette wheel produces the colours as an exact mirror image of this pattern. But how, these players reason, could the wheel come up with an exact mirror image of the predetermined order when this order is changed by players each day? In reality, of course, every order of red and black has the same probability.

The Labouchère system is also based on the idea that no loss is definitive. One simply notes the lost bet, and plays it again till it is won back. The routine prescribes that the bet size equals the sum of the two outer numbers of a number sequence. We start, for instance, with 1, 2, 3. The first bet is 1+3=4. If we lose, we add the lost bet to the sequence: 1, 2, 3, 4. Bet size is now 1+4=5. If we win this time, 1 and 4 are removed from the sequence: 2 and 3 remain. The play is continued till the whole sequence is crossed off. This system is related to the Martingale system. The difference is that the starting numbers can be chosen freely. In a conservative manner, like 1, 2, 1, or a daring game like 3,4,9.

The Fitzroy system is also based on the Martingale principle that previous losses can be made good through increase of the bet size. The goal is to win one unit in each round, and the play is stopped when this goal is reached. As long as the goal is not reached, even after winning a round, bet size is increased in step,via 1, 3, 4, 5, 6, ...and so on (2 is omitted). The limit is that bet size should never be larger than necessary for winning one unit per round. Imagine a sequence of losing four times, followed by three wins. The following bets and goals are obtained:

round 1: bet 1, lost, next goal 1+1 = 2
round 2: bet 3, lost, next goal 5+1 = 6
round 3: bet 4, lost, next goal 10+1 = 11
round 4: bet 5, lost, next goal 16+1 = 17
round 5: bet 6, won, next goal 11+1 = 12
round 6: bet 7, won, next goal 5+1 = 6
round 7: bet 7, won, next goal -1+1 = 0

In total 13 units are lost and 20 won, although only three out of seven rounds were won.

The D'Alembert system is based on the conviction that, in the long run, red and black must come out with the same frequency. Assume a simple series like: red-red-red-red-black-black-black-black.If a player bets on black all the time, he would have lost and won equally often. The D'Alembert system prescribes that one unit is added after a loss, and one unit subtracted after a win. Starting with one unit, the losses after four reds are 1+2+3+4 = 10. In the meantime the bet size has increased to five. The four wins are 5+4+3+2 = 14. Thus each pair of red and black yields a profit of one unit. The effect in a mixed series like: red-black-red-red-black-red-black-black is exactly the same. The bets are: 1, 2, 1, 2, 3, 2, 3, 2. The underlined bets, a total of 10, are won. The others, a total of 6, are lost. Again there is a snag in this system: it is not at all certain that reds and blacks will balance each other in the long run.

Wells' system is a variation on the system of D'Alembert. The difference is that one starts with a bet of 10 units, increasing or decreasing from thereon. The game is stopped, winning or losing, when bet size has reached either zero or 20.

Many other systems (e.g. Philiberte, Coups de Deux) are based on these same principles. The fallacy of all such systems is the assumption that successive bets can compensate each other. In reality all successive bets are independent events, and the expected loss is 2.7% for each or them (or 1.35% for simple bets), irrespective of bet size. A more elaborate proof of the futility of betting systems is provided by Epstein (1967).

OUTCOME VARIANCE

Although in roulette all bets on numbers have the same expected value, the spread among the outcomes is different. A bet b on a single number has as possible outcomes + 35 b or -b (36 times). The standard deviation is 5.84 b. A bet b on 12 numbers has as possible outcomes + 2 b (12 times) or -b (25 times), and a standard deviation of 1.40 b. The impact of this difference is clear when we consider a problem like how to win at least Dfl. 350 in roulette, when betting 73 times one chip of Dfl. 10. Placed on a single number the chance of winning at least three times is approximately 0.23. Placed on a simple chance (even counting the "in prison" rule), the chance of winning 54 times out of 73 rounds is infinitely small.

The example illustrates that the objectives of players may influence the playing strategy. Winning large sums with fixed bet sizes is possible only when the outcome variance is large. Of course the "risky" bets could also incur large losses. The probability of never winning in 73 rounds is 0.07 when single numbers are played, and again infinitely small for the simple chances.

Avoidance of large losses, or the objective of staying in the game as long as possible, leads to a preference for the less risky bets. Players who do not want to exclude the possibility of winning a large sum should prefer risky bets. Thus roulette offers the option of selecting different strategies, dependent on the objectives of individual players. In this chapter we will investigate how preferences for outcome variance are distributed among players. Two sources will be used: an instruction book on betting strategies (Terheggen, 1980) and observations in a casino.

"One Hundred Winning Moves"

Terheggen's book on betting strategies is called *One Hundred Winning Moves at Roulette*, and contains betting patterns "used and tested by experienced players." The purpose of the book is to educate beginners, and to help them use their capital optimally. Hence the betting patterns are supposed to reflect some of the preferences and wisdom of habitual roulette players.

The idea behind all suggested moves is that the outcome variance is not only determined by the number of cells covered, but also by differential covering. For example, compare the three options presented in Table 4.1.

A spreading of the bet across cells decreases the variance of the outcome (B compared to A), but this can be partly compensated by making the distribution uneven

TABLE 4.1
Three Ways of Betting Dfl. 10 at Roulette

	No. of Chips	Value of Chips (Dfl.)	Placed on No.	Expected Value (Dfl.)	S.D. of Outcome (Dfl.)
A	1	10	27	-10/37	58.78
B	1	5	27	-10/37	40.70
	1	5	28		
C	1	5	27	-10/37	45.77
	1	5	27,28		

(C compared to B). Thus the effect of the strategy demonstrated in C is that more numbers are covered without completely sacrificing the possibility of winning large amounts. The expected value of the move is, of course, independent of the betting pattern. The book supports distribution of bets among cells with the argument that outcome variance should be large, because an occasional large profit enables the player to compensate for a series of losses.

In the analysis we will assume that a player places a unit bet size of 1.0 in each round. Distributed over n equal-valued chips each chip has a value of $1/n$. When all chips are placed as single bets, the standard deviation of the bet is:

$$\varsigma = \sqrt{\frac{36^2}{37n} - \frac{35}{37} - \frac{1}{37^2}} \qquad \text{(Form. 4.3)}$$

We will designate the number of cells covered by m. Substituting m for n, formula 4.3 represents the smallest value of ς for each value of m. In Fig.4.1 this minimum standard deviation is presented by a solid curve. The maximum standard deviation is reached when infinitely small parts of the unit bet are used to cover 36 cells, while almost all of the bet is concentrated on the one remaining cell. In the limiting case the standard deviation approaches 5.84. This value is indicated by the solid horizontal line in Fig. 4.1. The area between these two lines represents the options open for selection of outcome variability.

Figure 4.1 illustrates that in the moves suggested by the instruction book, outcome variability decreases when more cells are covered. Concentration of bets helps when few cells are involved, but for larger numbers of cells the effect is negligible. Of the available room for variance only a small portion is used, which makes one wonder why the complicated betting patterns are chosen at all. An example of this problem is presented in Fig.4.2.

Ten chips are placed as three straight bets, three split bets, two street bets, and two square bets. The effect is that on the disc, 13 adjacent numbers are covered (6 to 33). The roulette book states that this is a cunning move with a "strongly progressive

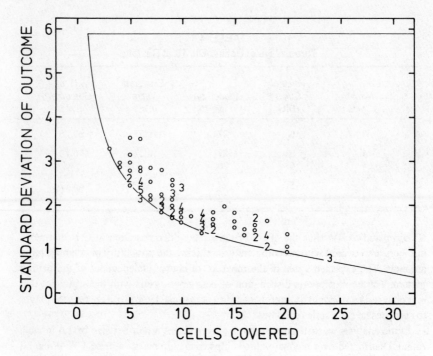

FIG. 4.1   Standard deviation and number of cells covered in instruction book on recommended bets. The drawn lines represent the theoretical minimum and maximum standard deviation.

outcome pattern," which means that some of the outcomes allow the player to continue the game for a long time. It is also advised that two players should place the chips, because of the complexity of the pattern. In fact 20 cells are covered with an outcome standard deviation of $\varsigma = 1.04$. Hence the pattern differs little from a simple chance. The major difference is that the simple chances have a much better expected value.

Observations on Players

Betting patterns of actual players were studied at the American Roulette tables in one of the Dutch state-operated casinos. American Roulette, the way it is played in The Netherlands, was chosen because all players have chips of their own colour. Hence confusion is reduced to a minimum. Another advantage is that each player has chips of one value only, which facilitates the difficult job of recording. A third advantage is that the number of players at each table is limited. The roulette table did not have the double zero, which exists in almost all casinos in the United States.

In total, 29 different players were observed. Observations started when players arrived at a table and acquired their own chips. Observations stopped when players left the table. The median number of rounds played in between was eight, ranging from one to eighteen. Each player can be characterised by the mean number of cells covered

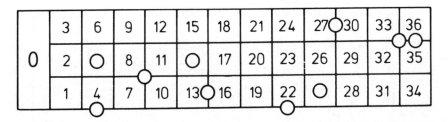

FIG. 4.2   A bet with 10 chips, covering 20 numbers.

and the mean standard deviation of outcomes. These mean values are representative of a player's strategy when little variation among rounds is observed. The round-to-round variance can be represented by the standard deviation of these two characteristic statistics.

All these values are represented in Fig.4.3. The circles represent the medians of all bets placed by each player. The horizontal and vertical bars indicate the standard deviation among rounds.

The first conclusion drawn from Fig.4.3 is that players differ widely with respect to the preferred outcome standard deviation, or the preferred level of risk. Almost the full range is utilised, although the main body of observations fall between standard deviations of 1.0 and 4.0.

Secondly it is shown that betting patterns have an almost even spread across cells, such that most players stay close to the lower limiting curve. Players select risk levels not by uneven distributions within the betting pattern, but by variation of the number of covered cells. Thirdly we find that the preferred risk levels are quite high, compared for instance to the outcome standard deviation in blackjack, which is for an average player only 1.03 times the bet size. The fourth conclusion is that 13 out of 29 players sometimes place bets covering between 15 and 20 cells. Such bets come close to the simple bets, like black-red, odd-even and high-low. One can wonder why such multiple bets are preferred to the simple bets which have a much better expected value because of the in-prison rule.

The fifth conclusion from Fig.4.3 is that variations within players were relatively small. For 18 out of 29 players represented in Fig.4.3(a), the intra-individual variance was negligible. The remaining subjects, represented in Fig.4.3(b), varied their bets somewhat more, but not according to a clear system. Table 4.2 reveals that these players tended to place less chips after losing, simultaneously increasing the risk level. This can be achieved only when after losing the number of cells covered is decreased.

The predominant tendency is against the family of strategies which attempt to win by increasing bet size after losing, such as the Martingale system. However, like in blackjack, the predominant strategy is not present in all bets, nor in all players. The outcome of the previous round is clearly not the only factor that determines the strategy. An illustration of this fact is presented in Table 4.3. This table shows that after winning, players tend to leave their bets simply on the table, as if they expected that the winning

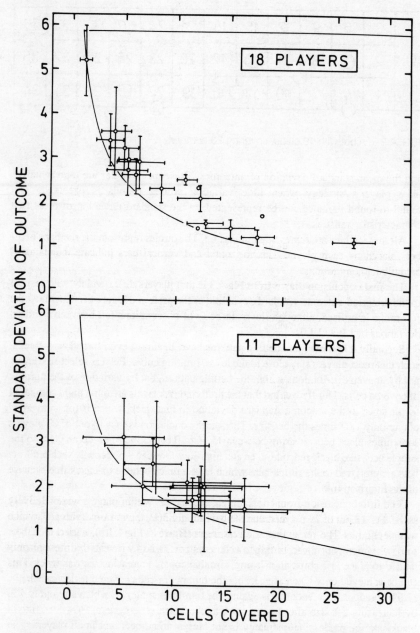

FIG. 4.3   Preferred standard deviation of the outcome. Each dot represents a subject. The horizontal and vertical lines represent the standard deviations within a subject. The subjects are divided over two figures in order to enhance legibility.

TABLE 4.2
Intra-individual Variations for the 11 Players Who Varied Their Bets Most

Preferred Strategy	After Winning Previous Play	After Losing Previous Play
Bets with increased risk	15	29
Bets with decreased risk	23	22
Bets with more chips	20	13
Bets with less chips	18	27
Bets with more cells covered	20	13
Bets with less cells covered	21	27

TABLE 4.3
Selection of Numbers in Roulette

Strategy	No. of Bets
After winning, staying on previous winning number	70
After winning, moving away from previous winning number	5
After losing, moving to previous winning number	5
After losing, staying away from previous winning number	70

number will come again. After losing they do not move their bet to the number which came up previously. Instead they place their bet on the numbers that lost previously, as if it is now time for these numbers to come up.

THE HOPE OF WINNING

The effect of a preference for bets with a moderate risk level is that players deprive themselves of the chance of ever winning a large amount. This is illustrated in Fig.4.4.

In this figure the individual dots represent possible outcomes at the end of 1, 3, 10, 30 or 100 rounds. It is assumed that the bets are divided over two numbers (A), which results in a risk level of 4.0; over 12 numbers (B), resulting in a risk level of 2.0; or over 18 numbers (C), resulting in a risk level of 1.0. The connecting lines are only added to aid the eye; they do not represent any real outcomes. On the vertical axis of Fig. 4.4 the probability is plotted of gaining at least the profit mentioned on the horizontal axis. Thus, when a bet is placed on two numbers, there is, after playing 100 rounds, a 17% probability of making a profit equal to or above 44 times the worth of each single bet. The right-hand shift of the curves represents the cumulative effect of playing more rounds. Thirty rounds represents one-and-a-half hours of playing, and one-hundred rounds means a full evening. The purpose of Fig.4.4 is to illustrate the devastating effect of a preference for bets on many numbers, i.e. for low-risk bets. Take

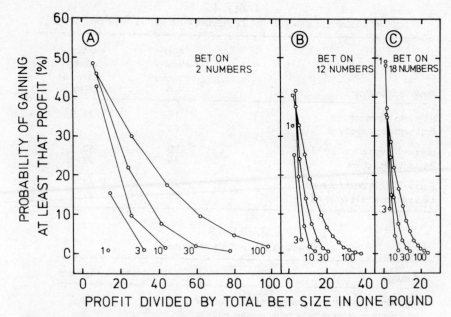

FIG. 4.4 The probability of winning at least the profit recorded on the horizontal axis. The dots represent possible outcomes after 1, 3, 10, 30, or 100 rounds. The lines do not represent possible outcomes. The bets are placed on two numbers (A), 12 numbers (B), or 18 numbers (C). These values represent the extreme risk level of S.D.= 4.0 (A) and S.D. = 1.0 (C). The median preferred risk level of S.D. = 2.0 is presented in box (B).

the example of a gambler who bets Dfl. 100 in each round with the purpose of winning Dfl. 1000 after 100 rounds. Betting on two numbers results in an almost 45% chance of achieving at least this goal. But spreading the bet across 18 numbers reduces the probability of achieving this, or a better result, to only 12%. The advantage of risky bets is of course offset by a higher probability of losing large amounts. Thus the choice of a strategy depends on the players' objectives. Players who want to win large sums should prefer risky bets. Players who want to avoid large losses, or to stay in the game as long as possible, should reject risky bets. The results presented in Fig.4.3 mean that roulette players do not, in general, play as if they want to win large sums. They may have the intention of winning large sums, but in that case experience should have taught them to reject their inappropriate strategies. Habitual gamblers can easily lose 100 times their average bet size each month. Their strategies reduce the chances that they will make up for this loss, on any particular visit, to almost zero, unless they increase the size of their bets. Table 4.4 reveals that increases of bet size are always moderately small. The large majority of gamblers varies bets by not more than a factor of five. The increases are invariably incidental, and only in about half of the cases follow a loss. Hence we can conclude that players neither attempt to win large sums by "playing risky bets," nor to compensate previous losses by sudden increases of bet size.

TABLE 4.4
Variation of Bet Size Within
Players

Ratio of Highest and Lowest Bet	Number of Players
1.0–1.9	7
2.0–2.9	11
3.0–3.9	2
4.0–4.9	2
≥ 5.0	7

CONCLUSION

Although the expected value of multiple bets is always the same, the choice between betting on few or many numbers allows the player to select from a variety of risk levels. The standard deviation of the possible outcomes of a bet ranges from zero to 5.84.

Players use the range from 1.0 to 4.0. Thus the game offers the variety of strategies sought by players. However, the option of changing risk levels is not fully employed by individual players. They seem to stick to their preferred strategy, independent of the course of the game. The strategies selected by most players do not give the prospects of large profits. Roulette players should not hope to win their money back, when they play as they do.

CHAPTER 5

Lotteries: Big Prizes and Small Expectations

In many countries participation in lotteries is extremely popular and less tainted than playing in casinos. This popularity is somewhat paradoxical when it is considered that in roulette-type games more than 95% of the amount bet is returned to the players, whereas in lotteries this proportion is usually below 50%. The Dutch State Lottery returns 35 million guilders out of a monthly revenue of 50 million. Thus the expected value is -30% of the bet. The Dutch Giro Lottery returns 3 million guilders out of a revenue of 12 million, thus offering an expected value of -75%. Compared to the expected loss of 2.7% in French Roulette, and 0.5% for Basic players in blackjack, the losses incurred in lotteries are huge. However the two major Dutch lotteries still attract 2 million and 1.2 million players monthly. Not only is this general attractiveness of lotteries miraculous, one should also wonder why the Giro Lottery, with its much larger expected loss can, so easily, compete with the State Lottery. Or conversely, why the State Lottery continues to return 70% of its revenue, when obviously a return of 25% would be sufficient to attract the players. Apparently this is a market for which the market mechanism does not work at all.

The distinctive features of many lotteries are:
- low cost of lottery tickets;
- infrequent opportunity of betting;
- long delay between bet and outcome;
- a few disproportionally large prizes; and
- a large number of small prizes.

The cost of lottery tickets is usually so low that buying one ticket could never be considered a major encroachment upon one's purse. It is also not possible to lose large sums by playing too often in a short period, like in roulette and other casino games. The major prizes are enormous, when compared to the size of the bet. In the State Lottery the first prize is half-a-million guilders, 20,000 times the size of a bet. The Giro Lottery has a prize of Dfl. 100,000, still 10,000 times the bet size. In roulette the maximum ratio in a single bet is 35. In repeated bets the lottery ratios can only be reached by an exceptional event like placing three successive straight bets on the correct number. The number of prizes in lotteries is usually also quite large: one million prizes for two million tickets in the State Lottery; 135,000 prizes for 1.2 million tickets in the Giro Lottery. The large majority of these prizes do not surpass the cost of a lottery ticket, however. In the State Lottery 80% of the prizes are less than, or equal to the cost of a ticket. In the Giro Lottery this accounts for 89% of the prizes. These numbers suggest that players are stimulated by the vision of winning a very large prize while investing only a small amount. The combination of small investments and big prizes could stimulate what has been termed the "gambling instinct" in American jurisprudence (see Chapter 6). The large number of small prizes may motivate people to go on buying tickets, despite the fact that they never regain their investment.

The question addressed in this chapter is what combinations of parameters produce lotteries that are attractive for gamblers. It is obvious that, contrary to normative expected value theory, there is no need to offer gambles with a positive expected value. But how poor can the expected value be? Is it possible to return, say, less than 10%, and still attract a crowd?

EXPERIMENTAL STUDY

Normative theory states that the attractiveness of gambles is fully determined by their expected value, i.e. :

$$EV = \sum_{i=1}^{N} p_i V_i - C \qquad \text{(Form. 5.1)}$$

in which V_i is the prize won when outcome i occurs; p_i is the probability that outcome i occurs; and C is the amount of money invested by buying tickets. The N outcomes are exhaustive and mutually exclusive. In principle a gamble should not be attractive when EV is negative. Thus the limiting condition would be EV ≥ 0, or

$$\sum_{i=1}^{N} p_i V_i \geq C \qquad \text{(Form. 5.2)}$$

In practice we know that all lotteries have a negative expected value, which does not prevent the participants from buying tickets. Several explanations for this violation of expected value theory have been put forward. One is that small probabilities are generally over estimated. This phenomenon is well-established, for instance by Slovic, Fischhoff, and Lichtenstein (1982). A problem of this explanation is that in lotteries probabilities are not made known to the public, because they depend on the number of tickets that are sold. Even worse, gamblers hardly ever seem to be interested in how many tickets are sold. Another explanation is that the original investment is discounted. Discounting previous expenditures is, as will be remembered, an option envisaged by Prospect Theory, which states that people compare their prospects of winning and losing, to their financial status quo. The status quo could be determined after the acquisition of the lottery ticket. Expected value, as expressed by formula 5.1, will always be postive if the constant C is discarded. A third explanation is that people like the kick, the excitement, maybe the suspense, of possibly winning a large amount. It is not the probability that counts, but the possibility. The study reported in this chapter will shed more light on these theoretical explanations.

The lotteries considered in this experiment have, unlike the State and Giro lotteries discussed above, only one size of prizes. The number of prizes may vary, but all prizes within a lottery have the same value. In principle the structure of such lotteries is determined by four quantities: C = the cost of a ticket; N = the number of tickets that are sold; n = the number of prizes; and V = the size of these prizes. The expected value of such lotteries is determined by:

$$EV = \frac{n \cdot V}{N} - C$$

(Form. 5.3)

For EV to be positive it is required that:

$$\frac{n \cdot V}{N} \geq C$$

(Form. 5.4)

The basic methodology employed is that three out of these four parameters are fixed by the experimenter, while the fourth is selected by the subjects. Thus one could ask: how many tickets would be sold if a lottery offers ten prizes of Dfl. 100,000, and the cost of a ticket is Dfl. 25? In this way there are four conditions, in which subjects produce estimates of C, N, n, and V, respectively. Within each of these conditions the three parameters selected by the experimenter can be varied, in order to determine how the fourth parameter depends on the value of the other three.

Instructions

Subjects received the following written instructions in Condition 1:

It is your task to organise a nationwide lottery. The idea is to sell, with the aid of advertising and TV commercials, as many tickets as is possible. There are only 10 prizes, each of Dfl. 10,000. As an organiser, you do not think that people are going to risk their money for charity. But if the cost of a ticket is right, they will. On the other hand, you do not want to make the tickets too cheap, because the profit should be maximised. What is, in your opinion, the right cost of a ticket, if you aim at a total sale of one million tickets?

Similar instructions were used in the other three conditions. In each instruction three parameters were stated by the experimenter, while the fourth was determined by the subjects. Twelve parameter combinations were used in each condition, through factorial combination of the values presented in Table 5.1.

In each condition a separate group of 200 subjects was employed. Two parameters were varied between subjects, and one within subjects, as indicated in Table 5.1. As a result each of the 12 parameter combinations within a condition were judged by 50 subjects. All subjects were students at a Dutch university.

Results of Condition 1: Judged Acceptable Cost

As an example, the results of Condition 1 will be fully discussed. The results of the other conditions can then easily be understood when presented summarily. The raw results of Condition 1 are presented in Table 5.2.

It is clear from this table that subjects have at least a rough understanding of how the parameter variations should affect the cost per ticket. When more tickets are sold, the cost per ticket drops. Since this parameter was varied within subjects, one could argue that this result was evoked by the demand characteristic of the experimental design. Some arguments against such an interpretation will be presented later on. The

TABLE 5.1
Parameter Values of the Four Conditions of the Lottery Study[a]

Condition	C (Dfl.)	N	n	V (Dfl.)
1	?	*10,000	1	10,000
		100,000	10	100,000
				1,000,000
2	10	?	1	*10,000
	25		10	100,000
				500,000
3	10	100,000	?	*1,000
	25	1,000,000		10,000
				100,000
4	10	*10,000	1	?
	25	100,000	10	
		1,000,000		

[a]A question mark means that this parameter was the dependent variable. Parameters marked with an * were varied within subjects. C = cost of lottery ticket; N = number of tickets sold; n = number of prizes; and V = size of prize.

TABLE 5.2
Acceptable Cost Per Ticket in Dfl., Estimated by Subjects in
Condition 1[a]

N = Tickets Sold	One Prize of 10,000	One Prize of 100,000	Ten Prizes of 10,000	Ten Prizes of 100,000
10,000	2.50	10.00	10.00	15.00
	5.00	15.00	15.00	100.00
	10.00	25.00	25.00	150.00
100,000	1.00	2.50	2.50	10.00
	2.50	5.00	5.00	15.00
	5.00	10.00	9.00	15.00
1,000,000	0.50	1.00	1.00	1.75
	1.00	2.50	1.00	2.50
	2.50	2.50	2.50	5.00

[a]The three numbers in each condition refer to the first quartile, median, and
third quartile scores in groups of fifty subjects.

reactions to variations in the other two parameters were also in the correct direction: the judged acceptable cost of a ticket rose with n = the number of prizes, and with V = the size of each prize.

A closer look at the reaction to parameter variations is provided by an analysis of variance on the log-transformed scores. This analysis revealed significant main effects of N, n, and V. None of the interactions among these variables reached significance, which means that the judged acceptable cost can be described by a multiplicative model such as described by formula 5.4. According to this formula the effect of decreasing N by a factor of 10 should be that the acceptable cost goes up by the same factor. Likewise the effect of increasing n and V should be that the acceptable cost increases by a factor of 10. A simple parameter fitting, based on ordinal conjoint measurement, shows that the median data can be described by the multipliers shown in Table 5.3. Since the ratios between first quartile, median and third quartile scores appear to be quite stable, multipliers describing the spread among subjects are also entered in Table 5.3.

One conclusion that follows from Table 5.3 is that subjects' reactions to the parameter changes are in the correct direction, but too small. This is also seen when median judged acceptable cost is expressed by a multiplicative relation with weighted parameters:

(Form. 5.5)

$$C = 12.2 * N^{-0.53} * n^{0.35} * V^{0.47}$$

This expression is the least squares fit to the data, within the restriction of the

TABLE 5.3

Multipliers Describing the Independent Effects of the Parameter
Changes in Condition 1

Parameter Change	Normative Theory	Data
Decrease of N from 100,000 to 10,000	10	3.4
Decrease of N from 1,000,000 to 100,000	10	3.4
Increase of n from 1 to 10	10	2.2
Increase of V from 10,000 to 100,000	10	3.0
First quartile to median	-	2.0
Median to third quartile	-	1.7

multiplicative relationship. The results of Condition 1 are also graphically presented in Fig. 5.1. The figure reveals that the outcomes of the fitted model (formula 5.5) are always within the interquartile range, and often quite close to the actual median.

The underreaction to changes in N, the parameter varied within subjects, is hardly less than the other two, which suggests that the demand characteristic of the experiment did not unduly influence the subjects.

The net effect of the undervaluation of the three parameters is in a way compensated by the multiplicative constant 12.2. This constant adjusts the grand mean of all judgements. It could be chosen low enough to render all conditions highly profitable for the players, or high enough to make them profitable for the organisers. Table 5.4

TABLE 5.4

Expected Values in Dfl. of the Lotteries in Condition 1, Relative to the
Acceptable Cost Per Ticket[a]

N = Tickets Sold	One Prize of 10,000	One Prize of 100,000	Ten Prizes of 10,000	Ten Prizes of 100,000
10,000	−60	0	0	+567
	−80	−33	−33	0
	−90	−60	−60	−33
100,000	−90	−60	−60	0
	−96	−80	−80	−33
	−98	−90	−89	−33
1,000,000	−98	−90	−90	−43
	−99	−96	−90	−60
	−100	−96	−96	−80

[a]The three numbers in each condition refer to first quartile, median, and third quartile, and are expressed in percentages.

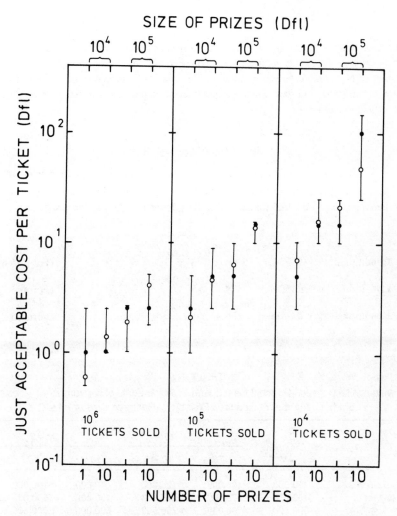

FIG. 5.1 Judged acceptable cost per ticket in Condition 1 of the lottery study. Presented are median scores (filled dots) and interquartile ranges. The open dots are the median outcomes of the fitted model.

illustrates that the constant is chosen too high: the expected values, relative to the highest acceptable cost specified by formula 5.4, is almost invariably negative.

Subjects are prepared to invest a median five guilders for a lottery ticket, irrespective of the fact that the median expected gain (not corrected for the cost of a ticket) is only one guilder. From the fact that variation in the parameter values of the lottery do not sufficiently change the judged acceptable cost, we may conclude that the overall cost of five guilders is not derived from the description of the lottery, but just from an anchoring point, representing the fair price of a lottery ticket. If this speculation about the origin of the multiplicative constant is correct, we should be able to observe similar results in the remaining three conditions. Asked about the acceptable values of N, n, and V, subjects should produce values that are normal in the lotteries they are used to, and that reflect the parameters of the experimental lotteries in an insufficient manner.

Results of Conditions 2, 3 and 4

The median responses in Conditions 2, 3 and 4 are presented in Table 5.5. The effect of parameter changes was in all instances less than prescribed by normative theory, as is demonstrated by the multiplicative relations describing the median responses:

Condition 2 $N = 656 * C^{-0.75} * n^{0.50} * V^{0.66}$ (Form. 5.6)

Condition 3 $n = 15.52 * C^{0.91} * N^{0.51} * V^{-0.86}$ (Form. 5.7)

Condition 4 $V = 0.87 * C^{0.51} * N^{0.84} * n^{-0.41}$ (Form. 5.8)

TABLE 5.5
Median Responses in Conditions 2,3, and 4: Judgements of N (Number of Tickets Sold); n (Number of Required Prizes); V (Required Size of Prizes)

	V	C=Dfl. 10		C=Dfl. 25	
		1 Prize	10 Prizes	1 Prize	10 Prizes
Condition 2:	10,000	100,000	125,000	10,000	100,000
Number of	100,000	275,000	675,000	100,000	500,000
Tickets Sold	500,000	500,000	1,750,000	500,000	1,000,000

	V	C=Dfl. 10		C=Dfl. 25	
		$N=10^5$	$N=10^6$	$N=10^5$	$N=10^6$
Condition 3:	1,000	100	1000	250	500
Number of	10,000	15	100	37	50
Required Prizes	100,000	4	10	4	10

	N	C=Dfl. 10		C=Dfl. 25	
		1 Prize	10 Prizes	1 Prize	10 Prizes
Condition 4:	10,000	10,000	2,500	10,000	10,000
Required Size	100,000	50,000	30,000	100,000	32,000
of Prizes	1,000,000	250,000	125,000	500,000	100,000

Analyses of variance on the log-transformed scores in each condition revealed main effects of the variables manipulated by the experimenter, but no interactions, which confirms that the scores can be described by multiplicative relations. The variations of experimental variables are insufficiently reflected in the exponents of the fitted parameter values, and this effect is present both when variables are between subjects and within subjects. Apparently the demand characteristics of the experimental design did not force subjects to produce responses in accordance with the normative rule. The underestimation of the impact of experimental variables is in agreement with our suggestion that subjects select a "fair" anchoring point, which is then insufficiently adjusted on the basis of the actual properties of the lottery.

The distribution of expected values in the four conditions of the study is presented in Fig. 5.2. Only 6% of the 2400 responses led to a positive expected value. Most of the subjects accepted expected values worse than -90% of their bets. It should be realised that these subjects were not representative of the general population. They were students, most of whom received a basic training in probability theory during their high school education.

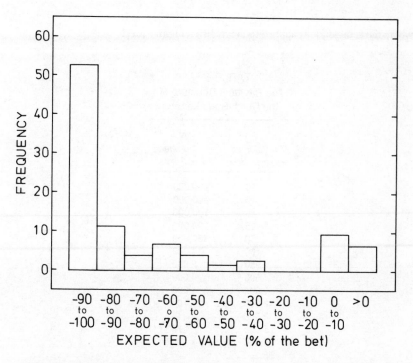

FIG. 5.2 Distribution of expected values of all responses in the four conditions of the lottery study.

VALIDATION

On the basis of our results it can be concluded that most people are attracted to lotteries with vastly negative expected values. Comparison between the results and existing lotteries is best achieved through formula 5.6. Usually people are informed about the cost of a lottery ticket, the number and sizes of prizes, but not about the number of tickets sold. The decision to buy a ticket is therefore based on C, n and V. In this situation the evaluation that subjects make could be described by formula 5.6. N should then be interpreted as a measure of attractiveness. The question is whether such an attractiveness score can be equated to the actual number of tickets sold. A tentative answer is obtained by comparing the computed N for existing lotteries to the actual sales of tickets. One problem is, however, that existing lotteries offer a large variety of prizes: a few very big prizes and many small ones. This is illustrated in Table 5.6, in which the payment structure of the Dutch State Lottery is presented. For this reason it is proposed to adapt formula 5.6 as follows:

$$N = 656 * C^{-0.75} \left[\sum_{i=1}^{m} n^{0.66} * V^{0.89} \right]^{0.75} \qquad \text{(Form. 5.9)}$$

where the summation is applied to the m different prize levels.

TABLE 5.6
The Payment Structure of
the Dutch State Lottery

V = Value of Prize in Dfl.	N = Number of Prizes
10	200,000
15	200,000
20	200,000
25	200,000
50	180,000
100	14,000
250	2,000
500	4,000
1,000	1,280
2,000	60
2,500	19
5,000	79
25,000	40
50,000	40
100,000	20
250,000	1
500,000	1

The rationale of this summation is as follows. We may split the compound lottery with m different prize levels, into m lotteries with only one prize level each. Assume that the cost of a ticket would be proportionally reduced to C/m, for each separate lottery. Then some of these lotteries would be more attractive than others. In the case of the Dutch State Lottery the least attractive partial lottery would contain 19 prizes of Dfl. 2500. The number of tickets sold would be, according to formula 5.6:

$$N = 656 * (1.47)^{-0.75} * (19)^{0.50} * (2500)^{0.66} = 374,484$$

The most attractive partial lottery contains 20 prizes of Dfl. 100,000, yielding a computed sale of 4,384,609 tickets. Only the most ardent gamblers would play in the least attractive partial lottery. Given a non-limited capacity for buying tickets, these ardent gamblers would also be attracted to the m -1 more attractive partial lotteries. If they acquire a ticket in each of the m lotteries, they are, in fact, buying a full ticket for the compound lottery. This minimum number of ardent gamblers can be increased by decreasing the differences between the partial lotteries. The maximum number of players willing to buy the compound ticket is found when the value of N is equal for all partial lotteries. This can be achieved by adjusting the cost of the partial tickets, under the condition that:

$$\sum_{i=1}^{m} C_i = C$$

Thus we find for all values of m,

$$if\ N_1 = N_2 = \ldots\ldots\ldots = N_m = N$$

$$then\ \ N = 656 * C_i^{-0.75} * n_i^{0.50} * V_i^{0.66}$$

$$or\ \ \ C = \left[\frac{656 * n_i^{0.50} * V_i^{0.66}}{N} \right]^{1.33}$$

$$or \sum_{i=1}^{m} C_i = 656^{1.33} * N^{-1.33} * \sum_{i=1}^{m} [n_i^{0.66} * V_i^{0.89}]$$

which is easily transformed into formula 5.6.

For the Dutch State Lottery the estimate of N, the number of tickets that could be sold, amounts to 2,033,698, which is very close to the actual number of 2,000,000. For the Giro Lottery the estimated value of N is 1,113,995, whereas in fact 1.2 million tickets are sold. Thus the predictive value of our laboratory results appear to be quite satisfactory.

Of course it is true that a full validation of formula 5.6 would require many more data points. Validation could also be obtained by verifying some predictions that follow from the formula. One prediction of formula 5.6 is that, given a constant sum of prize money, the maximum number of tickets will be sold when the total sum is spent on just one single but very large prize. In the case of the State Lottery a single prize of 35 million would yield sales of over 5.5 million tickets (not necessarily to an equal number of different players). It is, of course, questionable whether the formulae have any predictive value beyond the range tested in the experimental study, but the direction of the prediction is probably correct: the public is generally fascinated by lotteries with enormous prizes and low probabilities. This may be the reason why in other countries a much larger proportion of the prize money is concentrated in some of the big prizes. At the far extreme of only one enormous prize, something might go wrong, as was stated before by Friedman and Savage (1948).

Another aspect of the two lotteries under consideration is the large number of prizes that do not surpass the cost of a ticket. In the State Lottery 600,000 out of 2,000,000 tickets win prizes that are less than the ticket cost. In roulette it is only possible to win less than the original bet if one plays on the simple chances, and zero comes up. Instead of placing the bet "in prison" one sometimes has the option of losing half of the bet. No player would consider such a result a win. In lotteries this is different. The action of buying the ticket is, in time, clearly separated from the outcome. At the time the result is known, the expense of the lottery tickets may already have been incorporated in the status quo. This is another reason why lotteries have a long delay between buying tickets and the drawing of lots. A closer study of the function of these small prizes could be rewarding, since their contribution to the profit is, according to formula 5.6, less than the cost. The State Lottery should be able to sell about 1.8 million tickets if the 800,000 prizes of Dfl. 25 and below were eliminated. The result would be a sales decrease of Dfl. 5 million, but a decrease of Dfl. 14 million in prize money. The discrepancy between this computation and the usual inclusion of many small prizes in actual lotteries, might indicate that frequent winnings are necessary to ensure prolonged gambling. In that case formula 5.6 would apply to single lotteries, not to repeated ones.

CONCLUSION

I started this chapter by wondering about the popularity of lotteries, despite their enormous expected loss, and despite the vast differences among lotteries. The results of our study suggest that gamblers pay little attention to the actual properties of lotteries. This is already clear from the fact that they are not interested in the number of tickets that are sold, a dimension which is essential for the computation of expected value. The attractiveness of lotteries is determined much more by a comparison with tacitly accepted properties of a fair structure: the cost of a ticket should be relatively low, the lottery should offer prizes worth at least the price of a medium-price car. Within these marginal conditions it is unlikely that the participants will realise how poor their chances are. They like to win, but do not consider their probability of winning.

CHAPTER 6

Games of Chance and Games of Skill

This chapter is devoted to the legal problem of distinguishing between games of chance and games of skill. This problem is encountered in many countries, but became especially acute in The Netherlands, after the introduction of the game Golden Ten. With the exception of Great Britain, most national laws require judges to decide whether a game is a game of chance or a game of skill. The offering of a game of chance to the public, without a special licence, usually constitutes a violation of the law. The distinction between games of chance and games of skill leads to theoretical and practical problems and impossibilities.

In all games the outcome is determined by a mixture of chance and skill. The world chess champion could in a single game lose to a lesser player, just because he is tired, has a headache, or is distracted by a lady in a red blouse. It is possible to define skill in such a way that resistance against fatigue, illness and distraction are included. In that case, skill would be a continually fluctuating property. But usually the concept of skill refers to an underlying, more or less stable property that emerges when short-term variations are levelled off. When two top chess players like Karpov and Kasparov play 24 games, one player just does not win nor the other lose all the time. A world chess championship consists of 24 games, just to exclude the fluctuating elements, and to let the underlying small but structural difference of skill emerge. The same is true for bridge, soccer, tennis, and many other sports and games of skill. In the following we will assume that skill is a latent trait, and that playing the game provides a test of this skill, obscured by measurement error. We will call the component of error: chance. No game can ever be an error-free measurement of skill, hence every game involves a mixture of chance and skill. In this chapter I will discuss whether the two components can be usefully distinguished, and how this should be done.

In gambling the contribution of skill is reduced through the introduction of randomising devices like roulette wheels, dice and cards. The purpose of these devices is to minimise the skill component: the thrill of gambling is that the chances of winning are always present, even when you do not possess any relevant skill. On the other hand, elimination of skill is a guarantee needed by the house. When players can develop skills beyond levels envisaged by the designers of the game, it will become increasingly difficult to operate the game on a commercial basis.

The ideal skilled game, like ball games or chess, would be 100% dependent on skill, the ideal gamble 100% on chance. In reality the difference between the two types of games can be small, which makes it possible to bet on the outcome of skilled games, like soccer or horse racing. For legal purposes, however, the distinction between games of skill and games of chance is still useful, because in many countries these notions are used in laws regulating or prohibiting gambling. The distinction between games of chance and games of skill is, however, most important to the gambler. When gamblers attribute their losses to lack of skill, instead of to the odds of the game, they may never reach the conclusion that no amount of practice, and no change of strategy, will ever lead to a positive expected outcome. The practical difficulty of making the distinction on the basis of observed outcomes could present a basic obstacle. This I will illustrate by the example of soccer, a recognised game of skill.

THE WORLD SOCCER CHAMPIONSHIPS

The world soccer championships are played between 24 national teams. In the qualifying rounds six groups are formed, each with four teams of about equal strength. In each group of four all six possible matches are played, which leads to a total of 36 matches. This is of course a small number compared to the total of 256 that could have been played between all 24 teams. The disadvantage is that, if the three strongest teams are placed in the same group, number three will not make it to the semifinals. Spreading strong teams across groups will not fully eliminate this problem, because who knows in advance what the latent strength is? The two best teams in each group go on to the second round, in which 12 teams play. Four groups of three teams each are formed, and within each group all three possible matches are played. In the third round the four winning teams, A, B, C and D, are treated in a strange way. A meets B, C meets D, and the two winning teams play the final. When A and B are in reality the two strongest teams, it is unavoidable that the real number two ends up third or fourth. The composition of groups and the choice of opponents in the semifinals are determined by drawing lots. I have studied the effect of this random element by a Monte Carlo simulation (cf. Table 6.1). In this simulation error-free matches are assumed, which means that each match is won by the team with the greatest latent strength. The results presented in Table 6.1 show that, even in the absence of measurement error in matches,

TABLE 6.1
A Monte Carlo Study of the Effect of Drawing Lots in the World
Soccer Championships

Latent Strength	% Probability of Ending			
	First	Second	Third	Fourth
1	100	0	0	0
2	0	56	25	0
3	0	29	38	0
4	0	11	22	16
5	0	4	9	24
6	0	1	4	21
7	0	0	1	15
8	0	0	1	11
9	0	0	0	7
10	0	0	0	4

the wrong teams may finish second, third or fourth. Now, what happens if we add some measurement error in every match?

In principle we can only quantify the proportion of error if there is an underlying metric. We choose a ratio scale metric, on which the 24 teams are ordered with equal distances of scale value one. This scale represents the latent trait of strength, which is to be recovered through paired comparisons: the matches. Due to error the revealed strength is sampled from a normal distribution with the latent strength as mean, and a standard deviation sigma, which is the same for all teams (cf. Fig. 6.1).

The probability that team 1 will beat team 2 is again described by a normal distribution, with a mean equal to 1.0 (the difference between the means of team 1 and 2) and a standard deviation equal to two sigmas). When sigma equals 0.0 the probability that team 1 will beat team 2, or p(1>2), equals 100%. For sigma equals infinity p(1>2) becomes 50%. In general we can say that p(1>2) equals the area under the normal

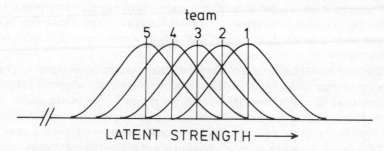

FIG. 6.1 A model of teams, ordered according to their latent strength, and measurement error added by actual games.

curve corresponding to z = 1/2 sigma. This probability can be expressed as a contribution of error to the total outcome by:

$$\text{proportion of error} = 2 - 2 \cdot p(1 > 2) \qquad \text{(Form. 6.1)}$$

where p(1>2) is the probability that team 1 beats team 2. The only unknown parameter of this model is sigma.

The way in which we estimate sigma is based on the assumption that in error-free paired comparisons, transitivity will be preserved in all triads. This was also the principle that underlay Lewis Carroll's proposal for optimal organisation of tennis matches (Carroll, 1883). If A beats B, and B beats C, transitivity requires that A will also beat C. However, when error is introduced in all individual comparisons, it can be that triads are intransitive. In the extreme, one quarter of the triads will be intransitive. Each group of four teams in the first round of the world soccer championships allows a test of four triads. The relation between the proportion of error and the number of intransitivities within a group of four teams is investigated again through a Monte Carlo analysis, involving a simulation of 80,000 championships. The result, presented in Fig. 6.2 (top panel), indicates that intransitivities occur rarely when less than 80% of the outcome is attributable to error. The reason is that a comparison of, for instance, team 1, 12, and 23 will lead to intransitivities only when team 23 beats team 1, or when 12 beats 1 *and* 23 beats 12.

The actual numbers of intransitivities in groups of four teams were counted in the world championships of 1930, 1950, 1958, 1962, 1966, 1970, 1974, 1978, 1982, and 1986. In total there were 43 groups of four, 172 triads and 30 intransitivities, or 0.17 per triad. Fig. 6.2 reveals that this relatively high number is reached when the proportion of error in a single match is 95%. The value of sigma corresponding to this error proportion is sigma = 6.25. Hence the realistic portrayal of soccer teams playing in the world championships is more or less as shown in Fig. 6.3. The latent differences among teams are small compared to the enormous variability due to influences not related to strength.

The effect of the large influence of error is revealed by Fig. 6.2 (lower panel). The probability of each team ending as world champion as a function of error proportion is again analysed by means of a Monte Carlo analysis. A more precise account is given in Table 6.2.

The conclusion is that chances of winning the championship are considerably spread over the stronger teams. Of course this is exactly why championships provide good entertainment. If it were close to 100% certain which team is going to win, there would not be so much public interest. A 95% influence of chance in each separate match is just right. But at the same time one should realise that the margin between a game of skill and a game of chance is extremely thin. Is it reasonable to assume that the outcomes will allow people to detect the difference between 95% chance and 100% chance?

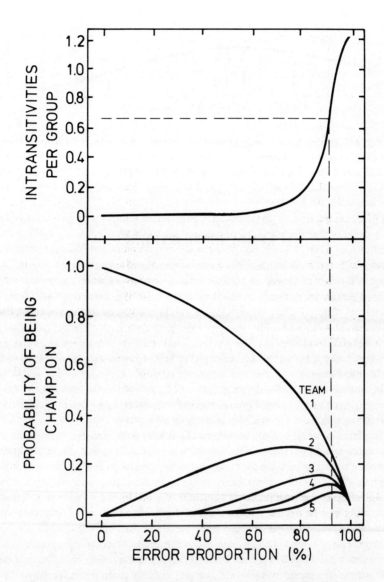

FIG. 6.2   Lower panel: the probability of winning the world soccer championships, as a function of measurement error. Upper panel: the number of intransitivities in a group as a function of measurement error. In practice, 0.7 intransitivities occur in a group. This means (upper panel) that the error proportion is about 95%. This proportion defines (lower panel) the chances of winning the championship.

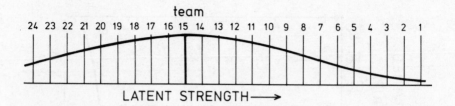

FIG. 6.3 All 24 teams arranged according to latent strength. For team 15 the probability distribution of strength measured by matches is sketched, on the assumption that the standard deviation is 6.25 times the unit distance between teams.

LEGAL DISTINCTIONS

A closer look at the difficulties gamblers may experience when they are required to distinguish games of chance and games of skill is obtained when we consider the problems legislators encounter when they try to make the distinction. All Western countries regulate gambling through legislation. In order to do that it is necessary to distinguish those forms of betting that need to be controlled, from other forms of betting which are considered harmless. The problem is rather tricky: in most countries playing poker for money is forbidden, whereas playing bridge for money is not. This issue is also highly relevant in the study of gambling, because a large amount of gambling research was inspired by the desire to solve the legal problem. Studies like the ones reported in Chapters 2, 3, and 4 were conducted with the explicit purpose of collecting material that could serve as evidence in the courtroom.

The definition of a game of chance should probably include roulette, craps, and all sorts of lotteries. But to simply enter into the law a list of forbidden games would not do, since it would be very simple to design a new game, or to give a new name to an old game. We need a more general definition that would also include games which do not yet exist. A broad definition of gambling was proposed by Devereaux (1968): "...gambling may be defined as a form of activity in which the parties involved, who are known as bettors or players, voluntarily engage to make the transfer of money or something else of value among themselves contingent upon the outcome of some future and uncertain event" (p. 53). It is clear that, according to this definition, offering prizes to the winner of a tennis match would also be gambling, since the victory is a future and uncertain event. What is lacking in Devereaux's definition is the distinction between chance and skill, and indeed most Western countries introduced this distinction in their legislation. However, once the distinction is introduced it raises the question of how in practice the two are to be told apart. Usually legislators specify that, in order for a game not to be classified as a game of chance, it has to be shown that skill is the predominant influence on the outcomes (e.g. Solomon, 1966). Again, this does not

TABLE 6.2
A Monte Carlo Study of the Effect of Measurement Error in the World
Soccer Championships

| Latent Strength | % Probability of Ending | | | |
	First	Second	Third	Fourth
1	23.7	12.7	11.9	5.0
2	18.3	12.0	12.5	5.4
3	14.7	12.1	11.2	6.1
4	12.1	10.8	10.1	6.7
5	8.8	9.7	9.4	7.2
6	6.3	8.6	8.6	7.2
7	4.8	7.7	7.2	7.1
8	3.5	5.9	6.5	6.4
9	2.4	4.8	5.2	7.3
10	1.7	3.9	4.2	6.4
11	1.2	2.9	3.1	5.8
12	0.9	2.4	2.6	4.9
13	0.6	1.7	1.9	4.4
14	0.4	1.5	1.4	3.8
15	0.3	1.0	1.3	3.3
16	0.1	0.7	0.9	2.9
17	0.1	0.4	0.8	2.7
18	0.1	0.5	0.3	2.0
19	0.0	0.2	0.3	1.7
20	0.0	0.2	0.2	1.0
21	0.0	0.1	0.1	0.8
22	0.0	0.1	0.1	0.7
23	0.0	0.0	0.0	0.6
24	0.0	0.0	0.0	0.4

solve the problem, because it is not clear what predominance means. The example of soccer championships is a sufficient illustration of the point: in a single match the influence of skill is very small indeed, but it would cause an uproar were soccer to be forbidden because the influence of skill is not predominant.

The central problem is how we establish that the procedure generating the outcome of a game, such as betting in roulette, or playing a soccer match, is or is not dependent on the actions of the players. Even in roulette this constitutes a problem, because winning or losing depends clearly on where the players placed their bets. The use of the roulette wheel does not exclude that players find a way of predicting the next outcome. Just calling roulette a game of chance because a wheel is used will not do. One should be able to show that, in the long run, the actions of the players do not affect the observed outcomes, and that the outcomes are equal to some value obtained through a formal analysis of the mechanics of the game.

Procedural Analysis

In principle there are two ways in which it can be shown that the players do not influence the outcomes. One is analysis of the procedure, the other is analysis of outcomes. Procedural analysis has led to the conviction that games such as lotteries and roulette are games of chance, because the players cannot influence the numbers that come out. Application of the same reasoning to card games, such as blackjack, poker and bridge, leads to obvious problems. Although the players cannot influence the order of the cards in a deck, they can still develop strategies that are optimal within the restrictions imposed by the cards. The skill of playing bridge or poker is not to receive the best cards, but to make the best of the cards received. The skill involved in blackjack is to tune the decision strategy optimally with respect to what is known about the cards remaining in the deck. Whether people are, in practice, able to develop strategies that help them to achieve better results, cannot be determined by an analysis of the mechanics of the game. Instead one needs an analysis of the psychological skills of players.

This conclusion backfires at the statement that lotteries and roulette are games of chance, because the question is not whether players can influence the selection of numbers, but whether they can develop optimal strategies, given the selection of numbers. Roulette is a perfect demonstration of this issue. On the basis of procedural analysis, roulette was considered as the game of chance par excellence for centuries. And indeed, if the equipment is well-balanced and calibrated, we will not find significant deviations from randomness in the number series. But this does not imply that the results of betting are also fully random. Many players believe that betting systems such as Martingale or d'Alembert will help to overcome the negative odds (cf. Chapter 4). Epstein (1967) demonstrated convincingly that such systems do not help the players, but the same author described another strategy that proffers a positive expectation, regardless of the precision of the roulette mechanism. This is how it works.

Before the ball is launched there is complete uncertainty with respect to the outcome, and each number has the same probability. At the end of the round, when the ball rests in one of the 37 compartments, the winning number has been determined, and all uncertainty has gone. Between these two states there is a gradually decreasing uncertainty; the transition from complete uncertainty to complete certainty is never abrupt. This means that between the launching of the ball and "rien ne va plus" the outcome will become predictable, unless "rien ne va plus" is called immediately. Indeed a prediction method has been developed, which utilises the gradual increase of information. The prediction is based on calculations involving physical parameters, such as the velocity of the ball and the wheel (which are supposed to be constant for one balleur), the point at which the ball leaves the rim, and the corresponding number on the wheel, and so forth. The extent to which the outcome is predictable depends on the ability of such players. Consequently, the nature of the game is no longer determined by the fact that the numbers are produced in a random fashion, but rather by the minds of those engaging in it. Procedural analysis will in this case not yield the desired distinction. The crucial question is whether people will be able to collect the information and to perform the computations described by Epstein. The nature of this problem is psychological. Sometimes legislators have tried to solve this problem by relying upon procedural analysis, unless it could be shown that a large majority of players did in fact develop a relevant skill. However, this implies that outcome analysis is needed additional to procedural analysis.

Outcome Analysis

Outcome analysis leads to even worse problems than procedural analysis. We might try to establish whether the results obtained by players are better than those which could be expected by chance. In the case of roulette this would involve testing whether players lose less than 1/37 of their bets. But chance levels cannot be computed for all games, without making some strong assumptions. In blackjack, for instance, a chance level does not exist independently of players' strategies, because the game can simply not proceed without the players taking decisions about hitting or standing, doubling, splitting, and insurance. One way to resolve this is on the basis of the assumption that these decisions are choices between two alternatives, such as hitting or standing, splitting or not splitting, and that both alternatives have a probability of 50%. On this assumption the chance level for blackjack appears to be a loss of 28% of each bet, but there is, of course, no logical ground on which such an assumption can be defended.

For games like poker and chess, in which players play one another, lack of influence on the part of the players would result in equal probabilities of winning. Apart from the fact that establishment of equality requires acceptance of the null hypothesis, we have seen that highly but equally gifted players will also win equally often. Hence the outcomes of such games only inform us about the differences between players, not about the absolute levels of their skills.

Measurement of skills of players is also problematic for a number of practical reasons. One is that casino managements are rarely happy with the idea that their clients will be observed in a rather obvious manner, because this might scare them off. Another reason is that the number of observations, collected for each player, depends on how long the players like to play. Quite often only a few games can be observed. It would be misleading to eliminate those short runs, because they are more likely to consist of losses, as losing is the most prominent reason to stop playing. A third problem is that small amounts of skill can only be detected in long sequences. The skill to overcome the 2.7% loss in roulette will be significant only after some 5000 rounds, because the chosen strategy introduces a standard deviation of 300% (cf. Chapter 4). There is just no way in which so much data could be collected for a single player. Is a skill that will reveal itself only after 5000 games too small to be considered as predominating? Or does the fact that the skill overcomes the odds favouring the house, and that a fortune can be won in this manner, imply predominance?

PLAYERS' PERCEPTION OF SKILL

I went into the problem of distinguishing games of chance and games of skill in a legal context, because it illustrates the insurmountable problems faced by players who want to base their decision to play on the same distinction, but without statistical assistance. Again a player possesses two principal ways of making the distinction: analysing the procedure of the game, or analysing the outcomes, and there is no reason to assume that players would be more successful than the legislators. Additionally players could consider how much effort they expend, or how much learning is involved. This might help to establish that chess playing is a skill, even when two chess champions beat each other equally often. However, there are strong indications that people are prepared to expend effort, even when it is to no avail, and that in these cases they tend to overestimate the impact of their effort. The studies by Langer (1975) on the illusion of control illustrate this point (cf. Chapter 8). Another illustration is the study by Oldman (1974), which revealed that roulette players consider the game as an exercise in skill, which consists of the construction and adaptation of prediction models. Some more subjectively experienced elements of skill in roulette were mentioned in Chapter 4. On the other hand we know that some skills, like speaking, reading or riding a bicycle, hardly require any conscious effort. For all these reasons it is not clear at all that the subjective experience of effort is a reliable measure of the application of skill.

The amount of training required to play a game is contaminated by the same problem. Surely players can register how long they have exercised, but again they lack an objective assessment of the effect of training. Blackjack players repeatedly explained to me that the decisions prescribed by the Basic strategy are only made by inexperienced players (cf. Chapter 2). Experienced players make conservative decisions, thereby increasing their losses, but apparently they are unable to assess this negative effect of experience. A similar phenomenon occurs in roulette. Experienced players acquire a large number of complicated betting patterns, but the expected value of all these patterns is exactly the same.

Notwithstanding all these problems it is not very likely that players would be unable to detect differences among games. It would be interesting to know, though, how they place games along the dimensions of chance and skill. Therefore my colleague Gideon Keren and I ran a simple experiment in which we asked students to scale games and sporting activities on a number of dimensions. The games and dimensions are presented in Table 6.3. There were two sets of nine games, and each set was administered to a different group of subjects. Three of the games were present in both sets. The two sets were combined through the use of these anchoring points. Blackjack was not included because it was felt that not all subjects would know enough about it. It was assumed that the other games and activities would be familiar enough to all subjects, even when they did not engage in them regularly. The number of subjects in Groups 1 and 2 were 103 and 104 students, respectively. The ratings were made on seven-point scales, marked "extremely relevant" on one side, and "no relevance at all" on the other side.

The experiment produced a 12 x 12 correlation matrix. As expected, some scaling

TABLE 6.3
Conditions of the Scaling Experiment on the Perception of Aspects of Games

Games		Scaling Dimensions (Both groups)
Group 1	Group 2	
1. Whist	1. Bridge	a. Amusement
2. Poker	2. Poker	b. Attractiveness
3. Tennis	3. Soccer	c. Honesty
4. Monopoly	4. Monopoly	d. Luck
5. Snakes & ladders	5. Ludo	e. Consequences
6. State Lottery	6. Roulette	f. Cosiness
7. Checkers	7. Chess	g. Intelligence
8. Car rally	8. Motor racing	h. Risk
9. Football pool	9. Football pool	i. Chance
		k. Training
		l. Skill
		m. Predictability

dimensions were highly correlated. Here are some examples.

Training and skill $r = 0.84$

Luck and chance $r = 0.70$

Amusement and cosiness $r = 0.67$

Intelligence and skill $r = 0.56$

Some of the correlations were highly negative:

Chance and training $r = -0.58$

Chance and skill $r = -0.55$

Luck and training $r = -0.48$

Luck and skill $r = -0.44$

These numbers indeed suggest a separation of chance and skill related variables. The scores were analysed by the Princals program (De Leeuw & Van Rijckevorsel, 1979), which performs an analysis of principal components (cf. Chapter 3). The games are points in a multi-dimensional space, whereas the scales are presented as vectors on which the stimulus points are projected.

Figure 6.4 reveals a clear dimension representing the distinction between chance and luck on one side, and skill, training, and intelligence on the other side. Perpendicular to this dimension is a second one, which seems to be more related to objectives of players: important consequences and high risk on one side, amusement on the other side.

Figure 6.5 reveals how the games project on the chance-skill dimension. There is a clear distinction between lotteries, casino games and board games involving dice on the left side, versus racing, sports and intellectual games on the other side. People have a feel for the extent to which they can influence the outcome of a game, at least in a

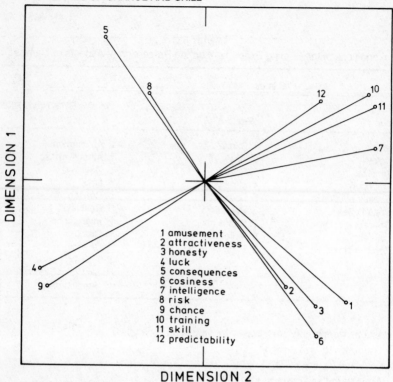

DIMENSION 2

FIG. 6.4   Results of Princals analysis: the vectors representing the 12 scales of judgement.

relative fashion. They do not confuse roulette with tennis, poker with bridge, or football pools with football. But roulette is not in the extreme position that is occupied by lotteries. Apparently a certain degree of skill is thought to be involved in roulette.

Being Attracted by the Reward Structure

The results presented in Fig. 6.5 support two conclusions. Firstly, that people have a feeling for the chance-skill dimension. And secondly, that games are not only characterised by the chance-skill dimension, which is related to the mechanism by which the winners of a game are selected, but also by the consequences, or the reward structure.

The first conclusion reveals that insensitivity to the chanceskill dimension is not the reason why people engage in gambling, despite its negative expected outcome. They could well know that a gamble involves little skill, or that they do not possess the required skill. Still they could be willing to wager money if the reward structure is such that prizes can be won without the use of skills. Let me give an example. It would be utterly foolish to enter a chess championship unskilled in chess playing, simply hoping that one would win by chance. There is no chance that someone, not possessing that

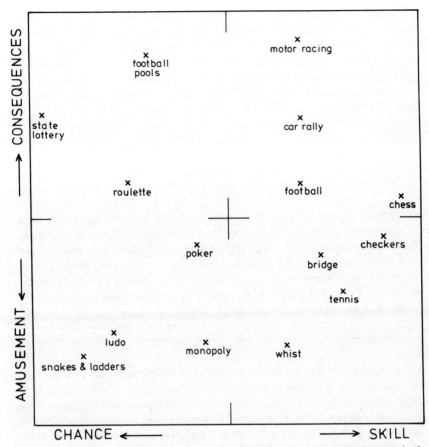

FIG. 6.5   Results of Princals analysis: the positions of 14 games and sports in the plane defined by chance vs. skill, and amusement vs. consequences.

skill, would win a chess championship, or even one single game. But the game of bridge is already different. Without the skills of a top player one will never win a top tournament, but a novice could win one single hand, simply by having the right cards. Therefore, if the reward structure is right, betting on a single hand could be attractive, even when skilled players have better chances. The public's ability to distinguish games of chance and games of skill is irrelevant when the attractiveness of games is more determined by the reward structure, than by the mechanism by which the winner is selected.

Notwithstanding the large individual differences in motivation for gambling, it is true that money constitutes one of the most potent rewards, sought by all gamblers (cf. Chapter 3, and Cornish, 1977). The literature on the chance-skill distinction has, to a large extent, neglected the aspect of the reward structure, and the fact that a reward structure could turn a skilled game into a gamble. There is one verdict by the Montana Supreme Court (State of Montana vs. Kilburn, 1941) that stressed this point: "an innocent game involving the element of skill alone becomes a gambling device when players bet on the outcome. To illustrate: A game of poker may involve more skill than chance and is innocent when played for pastime and amusement, but constitutes gambling when played for money" (p.103). According to this view the wagering of money becomes the necessary and sufficient condition for gambling. The contribution of skill is irrelevant, presumably because people could feel attracted to wager money in poker, even when they do not possess the necessary skills. This idea is further elaborated in the notion of "gambling instinct," mentioned in various court rulings (cf. American Jurisprudence 1968, and references there). The idea is not to embed gambling into an instinct theory of motivation, and therefore the term "instinct" was badly chosen. What the judges meant by "gambling instinct" is the willingness to wager money when the payment rule is unfavourable compared to the possible contribution of one's skills. This willingness is elicited by some aspects of the reward structure. The most important aspect of reward structures that invoke the "gambling instinct" is that the mechanism used for the distribution of prizes is such that all participants have about equal chances irrespective of their skills, or at least that novices perceive their chances as reasonable. Further it is necessary to promise the payment of money, or of highly desirable commodities. Within these conditions there are two aspects that are used separately or together: the frequent payment of small prizes, and the rare payment of enormous prizes.

The frequent payment of small prizes is encountered in casino games like roulette, blackjack and craps, but also in many lotteries. When players have a choice, like in roulette, many seem to prefer the frequent small prizes to occasional large ones. Most commercial lotteries pay huge numbers of very small prizes, usually even smaller than the cost of a ticket. A variation on this theme is the hall filled with slot machines, where individual players are not only receiving frequent but small rewards, but where the payment of rewards is ever present as an auditory avalanche of rattling money. The effect of frequent winnings is that players can be ahead of the house for long periods of time. To illustrate the point I calculated the probability of coming out equal to or ahead of the house after ten rounds, for blackjack and roulette (see Table 6.4). Obviously, the probabilities decrease as the number of rounds increases; in the long run all these probabilities, except for blackjack counters, approach zero. Research by Tversky and Kahneman (1971) demonstrated that people are insensitive to differences in sample size, and often regard the results of small samples as being representative of large samples. Looking at the effect of frequent winning in small samples one will come to the conclusion that the odds of the game are quite good.

The rare payment of enormous prizes is encountered in lotteries, football pools and television shows. Usually the prizes are so large that the win alters one's life fundamentally. Thus the owner of a chance of winning such a prize can cherish a fantasy about how one's life would change, and how all previous losses would be made good.

TABLE 6.4
The Probability of Coming Out Equal To, or
Ahead of the House, After Ten Rounds

Type of Game	Probability
Blackjack	
Card counters	0.65
Basic	0.62
Average players	0.56
Roulette	
Betting on simple chances	0.59
Betting on six numbers	0.50
Betting on one number	0.24

Especially for compulsive gamblers this is the only scenario that leads to a solution of their problems, which is one of the reasons why many compulsive gamblers return to their old habit after a treatment that initially looked successful (Fonteijn, 1985).

Stimulation of the gambling instinct is possible in all games with uncertain outcomes. If skill does not remove uncertainty completely there will always be the opportunity of designing a reward structure that promotes the idea of winning by chance. The conditions necessary for stimulation of the "gambling instinct" are a probabilistic nature of the outcomes, and appropriate reward structures. This, in practice, places gambling in the upper left quadrant of Fig. 6.5. But there is no reason why an adroit change of the payment rule could not turn all other games, even bridge, tennis, and chess, into something that would be attractive to gamblers. The chance-skill dimension is irrelevant when it comes to a definition of gambling: the reward structure is decisive.

Suggested Skill

In Fig. 6.5 games and sports are ordered along the chance-skill dimension, which means that people are sensitive to this distinction. But it is not implied that people perceive at the extreme left, where lotteries and roulette are positioned, a total absence of skill. On the contrary, I will argue that people find it very difficult to appreciate the probabilistic nature of the outcomes, and the total absence of skill, because they always tend to attribute at least part of the outcomes to their own actions. There is a widespread phenomenon, called the fundamental attribution error (Heider, 1958): people tend to attribute successes to their own actions, and failures to other influences. When gamblers win, they may try to determine what they did right this time. More about this is said in Chapters 7 and 8. At this moment I will only refer to the example of roulette. In roulette, players are encouraged to record the numbers that have come out, to perform computations, and to follow betting systems. The extremely complicated betting patterns, discussed by Terheggen (cf. Chapter 4), all having different names which are used in the instructions to the croupier, reinforce this suggestion of expertise. A large number of players do indeed believe that their results depend on personal skills (Csikszentmihalyi & Bennett, 1971). In the case of roulette the skill factor is more apparent than real, and the game is a perfect example of the illusion of control (Langer, 1975).

Legal battles about the chance-skill dimension refer to chance and skill as influences that can be established in an objective manner. The irrelevance of this dimension does not mean that the subjective perception of presence or absence of the influence of skill is also irrelevant for the acceptance of gambles. Rather the contrary is true: the subjective perception of a possibility of influencing the outcome could be essential, especially for the prolongation of gambling despite repeated losses.

GOLDEN TEN

In the section on the "gambling instinct," it has been argued that the chance-skill dimension, which refers to the way in which the winners of a game are selected, is irrelevant for a legal definition of gambling. Even when people can influence the outcome of a game, they could be invited by the reward structure to accept an unfavourable expected outcome. We know which aspects of the reward structure invoke this "gambling instinct": a reasonable chance of winning for all participants, monetary rewards, frequent small prizes or rare enormous prizes. In the present section I will apply this concept to the case of Golden Ten, a game that experienced an unexpected but excessive growth in The Netherlands.

Golden Ten is a pseudo roulette, designed to allow a certain degree of skill on the side of the players. As described in the section on legal distinctions, in the game of roulette it can be predicted where the ball will land, when its course is carefully followed. In Golden Ten this possibility is enhanced in four ways: there are no spoilers in the bowl; the bowl has a shallower slope, so that the descent takes a considerable time; the inner ring containing the numbers does not rotate; and there are two rings engraved in the bowl, which present a fixed reference.

It was claimed that this design enables players to make reasonable predictions, and indeed this claim was confirmed in a laboratory study. Subsequently about 150 casinos were opened throughout the country, returning a total net profit of at least Dfl. 200 million a year. The Dutch government fought these enterprises in the law courts, and the legal arguments focussed upon the distinction between games of skill and games of chance. Many of the ideas presented in this chapter were developed for this discussion.

It was clear that some players of Golden Ten can develop skills that enable them in a laboratory situation to make a proportion of correct predictions which lies far above chance level. But the nature of the psychological processes involved in producing the prediction rules is independent of the payment rule. The house could easily design a reward structure that does not even allow skilled players to make a profit. Producing the prediction would remain a skill, but the skill would not be great enough to compensate for the unfavourable odds. The acceptance of the bet would therefore depend on the payment rule, not on the efficacy of skill. The real question is whether the design of the game is such that players would accept a payment rule that is unfavourable compared to the level of their skills. Or, in other words, whether the design of the game stimulates the "gambling instinct" of those whose skills do not match the negative odds, specified in the payment rule.

The simplest answer is that this is, indeed, the case when the house makes profits. However, in court it was argued that the total profit of a casino could have come from one oil sheikh losing a few millions in one evening. It is possible that these millions compensated for the payments made to all other players. In that case one cannot maintain that the payment rule does not reflect the skills of most players. The question can only be settled by observations in casino conditions, such as presented in Chapters 2 and 4. The practical stumbling block is that casino owners would not welcome such observations. In one casino near the city of Nijmegen, the police were invited to make the observations, apparently because the owner trusted the outcome would be favourable for him. A total of 245 players were observed. Unfortunately the police recorded only how many rounds were won or lost, not how much money changed hands, nor on how many numbers the players were betting. Since the frequency of winning is uninformative in itself, these results can never lead to a conclusion. The police recorded also whether or not players followed the ball with their eyes during its descent. The idea was that the skill can only be used by observation of the ball, and that those who did not watch were gambling. Out of 245 players 65 always watched. They won 24% of their bets, on the average. Another 62 players never watched, but they still won 26% of their bets. These numbers clearly suggest that observation of the ball does not, in practice, increase the predictability of the outcome. The discrepancy with the laboratory results could stem from the adverse lighting conditions, the occasional change of balls, the regular cleaning of the bowl with some rinsing fluid, and the effects given to the ball by the balleur. But again, the number of plays won is somewhat uninformative. Players place their bets while observing the ball. It is possible that when they were uncertain they decided to place smaller bets. The effect of skill would then not be that they lost less bets, but only that they lost smaller bets, just like in the case of card counters at the blackjack tables.

Could any set of observations settle the question of whether Golden Ten is a game of chance? The problem focusses on measurement of the amount of skill employed by each individual player. A priori we can already state that no player will always win, or always lose. Commercially operated games are, by way of the proper mix of chance and skill, designed to cause interest and excitement. Casino games and other gambling games do not differ in this respect from typical games of skill. The probabilistic nature of games is a condition for their existence, but obstructs the accurate characterisation of their nature. Within a reasonable observation period it cannot be determined to what extent Golden Ten players use skills.

The police cannot do it, and neither can the players. The suggestion that Golden Ten is a game of skill may cause players to attribute occasional positive outcomes to skills that do not really exist. Hindered by such hindsight attributions, players will find it extremely difficult to discover that their efforts do in reality contribute little or nothing.

A more fruitful direction is to look at the reward structure of Golden Ten. It is a game with 24 numbers and two zeros. The payment rule is:

$$V = \left(\frac{24}{n} - 1\right) * b$$

(Form. 6.2)

in which V is the payment, n represents on how many numbers the winning bet was placed, and b is the size of the winning bet. It should be noticed that this formula is the same as the one described for roulette (formula 4.1). Assuming that the reward structure of normal roulette elicits the "gambling instinct," we must conclude that the reward structure of Golden Ten has the same potency. Gamblers accepting the negative odds in roulette without a chance of influencing the outcome, would also be willing to play Golden Ten, without the application of any skill. Playing Golden Ten constitutes gambling because its reward structure elicits the "gambling instinct."

CONCLUSION

Every game that invokes the interest of players combines the influences of chance and skill. Therefore a clear distinction between games of chance and games of skill cannot be made. Gambling is not restricted to those situations in which skill cannot be used at all. Rather we should define gambling as an overestimation of skill, relative to the odds provided by the reward structure of a game. The rejection of unfavourable gambles depends critically upon a correct perception of the structure of a game, and of personal skills. People tend to overrate the influence of skills, and this is not limited to gambling situations, as was demonstrated in the case of soccer championships. Therefore it should not surprise us that gamblers accept payment rules that cannot be compensated for by their skills.

CHAPTER 7

Chance and Luck

Few ideas are so deeply engraved in our minds as the notion that events have their causes. The existence of causelessness is so alien to us that in the absence of a known cause we tend to attribute events to abstract causes like luck and chance. In the domain of classical physics, luck and chance have no place. At its best such notions could be defined in terms of absence of knowledge on which the prediction of future events could be based. The throw of a dice, the spinning of a roulette wheel, or the shuffling of cards are considered to be chance events, not because they have no physical causes, but because there is insufficient knowledge to predict their outcomes. Chance is not a cause itself, but only alludes to the fact that the physical causes are unknown (cf. Keren & Wagenaar, 1985).

In the minds of many people luck and chance often seem to act as real causes. The physical influences which determine the behaviour of the roulette wheel ensure, through the multitude of coincidences, that all outcomes are equally probable. This aspect of equal probability, which is just another way of expressing the absence of knowledge relevant for prediction, suggests to many people that chance operates as a fair and balanced distributor which produces all possible outcomes with equal frequencies in the short run. The well-known gambler's fallacy, the belief that "tails" is more probable than "heads" after a sequence of successive "heads," is a direct consequence of the understanding of chance as a cause. Many related psychological phenomena are described as "the representativeness principle" (Kahneman & Tversky, 1972), "the law of small numbers" (Tversky & Kahneman, 1971), "sequential response bias" (Wagenaar, 1972), "subjective randomness" (Wagenaar, 1970). The general finding is that people expect small samples to be representative of large populations.

If the samples are drawn sequentially, this representativeness is brought about by an excess of alternations. In a sequence of heads and tails, people expect many short runs and no long runs, because a long run would upset the local representativeness of the sequence.

An experimental demonstration of this principle is provided by Wagenaar (1970). Strings of 50 white and 50 black dots were constructed such that the probability of repetition was varied systematically from 0.2, 0.3, 0.4, 0.5, 0.6, 0.7 up to 0.8. Examples are presented in Fig. 7.1. Sixteen different strings were prepared for each level of repetition probability.

In each of 16 successive trials subjects saw 7 strings, one of each level. Subjects were told that the strings were meant to represent possible outcomes of 100 flips of a coin. The task was to indicate which of the strings was most likely to be the one really produced by flipping a coin. In total 203 subjects indicated their preferences. For each subject a median response across the 16 trials was computed. The results are presented in Table 7.1. A large majority of 86% of the subjects prefer a low probability of repetition, or too many too short runs.

When people are confronted with sequences of wins and losses in roulette, blackjack, or other games they will usually not fail to notice the unexpectedly high frequency of longer runs. Far from adjusting their concept of what could happen by chance, they now invoke a second causal factor: luck. Someone who is lucky will win many times in succession; the same will happen when it is your lucky day, your lucky number, lucky colour, lucky table, lucky dealer (cf. Cohen 1960). The effect of good luck is to produce longer sequences of winning, the effect of bad luck to produce long streaks of losing. The relatively long runs in continued gambling might, therefore, easily be attributed to luck and bad luck, operating independently of chance. In this perspective luck and chance are two different and possibly interfering causal factors, underlying the occurrence of events.

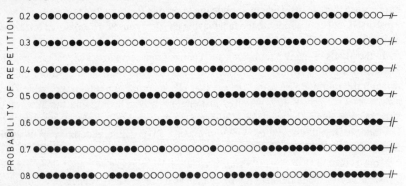

FIG. 7.1   Strings of 50 black or white dots, representing different probabilities of repetition. In the experiment each string contained 100 dots (50 black and 50 white). Subjects report that p = 0.3 or 0.4 looks the most random, which implies a preference for alternation.

TABLE 7.1
Repetition Probability in Strings of
Heads and Tails That Look Most
Random to Subjects (Wagenaar, 1970)

Probability of Repetition	Raw	No. of Subjects (Cumulative %)
0.20-0.25	8	4
0.25-0.30	20	14
0.30-0.35	38	33
0.35-0.40	43	54
0.40-0.45	32	69
0.45-0.50	34	86
0.50-0.55	22	97
0.55-0.60	2	98
0.60-0.65	4	100

The first indication that luck and chance are different and possibly complementary was obtained in a study on gambling (cf. Wagenaar, Keren, & Pleit-Kuiper, 1984; Keren & Wagenaar, 1985) in which many players were interviewed about various aspects of gambling. One of the questions was related to the degree to which the outcome of a gamble can be related to chance and skill (cf. Chapter 6). In our own perspective, chance and skill were the two factors that together account for the results of any game. Therefore we requested our subjects to split 100% into two parts, one indicating the influence of chance, the other the influence of skill. Our subjects seemed uncomfortable with this task, and only after extensive interviewing we realised that, in their opinions, there were really three factors. The third one was *luck*, and they had great troubles in deciding whether luck was more like chance than like skill. From a subsequently designed questionnaire we learned that one cannot force luck to happen. You should wait till luck appears, and in that sense it is much like chance. On the other hand you can lose your luck easily by using it unwisely. You can also fail to utilise it when it happens, for instance by not even noticing that this is your lucky day, or your lucky deck, or your lucky dealer. Finally, one can also ruin the effect of good luck by not noticing that it ended, thus losing everything that was won. In this sense the utilisation of luck is more like a skill. The special nature of luck explains why it is difficult to attribute the outcome of gambles to chance or skill only. When subjects were asked to divide 100% over three causal factors, chance, skill and luck, the following results were obtained (Keren & Wagenaar, 1985): chance 18%; skill 37%; and luck 45% (the mean of 22 judgements).

The message is quite clear: in the minds of gamblers, chance and luck are different causal concepts, both determining the outcomes in their own way. Luck, in this context, seems to be even more important than chance. Are chance and luck also perceived as different causes of events in daily life, or is the singular role of luck restricted to the population of gamblers in a casino entourage? In this chapter I will present two experiments, addressing this problem. In the first experiment subjects were asked to describe an event in their own life which they would consider a good example of chance (or luck, in another group). A new group of subjects scaled 80 of such stories on 12 dimensions, roughly like in a semantic differential technique. The scaled responses were then subjected to a discriminant analysis, in order to establish whether the luck stories could at all be distinguished from the chance stories, and, if so, to determine along which dimensions the two differ.

The second experiment employed a cover story technique (Wagenaar, Keren, & Lichtenstein, 1986). Cover stories were constructed that described some surprising event. The stories varied along the dimensions yielded in the first experiment: *surprise* and *consequence* of the outcome. In addition the amount of *superstitious reasoning* was manipulated as an experimental variable. The task of the subjects was to indicate, for the various stories, to what extent the events could be related to chance (one half of the subjects) or luck (the other half of the subjects). Because of the problem of story specificity, four different stories were constructed for each condition. The two experiments are described in greater detail in Wagenaar and Keren (1988).

DISCRIMINATION OF CHANCE AND LUCK IN DAILY LIFE

Story Construction

In the preliminary stage, 200 subjects, students at the Leiden University, were asked to write a short description of an event that happened in their own lives. One hundred subjects were asked to write a story that was a good example of something that happened by chance. The remaining subjects were asked to present a good example of a lucky event. Not all stories were suitable for subsequent use, which meant that a selection had to be made. The selection was achieved by exclusion of stories that met at least one of the following criteria: too short descriptions (e.g. one-liners like "I won a prize in a lottery"); incomprehensible descriptions; or descriptions that were, contentwise, very similar to other ones (e.g. meeting someone from your own neighbourhood in a distant country, or getting high grades in a test without really preparing for it). In fact similarity of descriptions occurred so often that there were almost always two stories that matched quite well. By selecting one of the two it was ensured that the selection did not alter the variability within the corpus.

After selection 80 stories remained, 40 representative of chance, 40 of luck. These stories were rewritten in order to achieve equal length, to remove slang, bad grammar, mis-spellings, personal detail, and all references to concepts used as scaling dimensions.

Method

All stories were to be scaled on the following 12 dimensions:
1. Important consequences
2. Luck
3. Escape from negative consequences
4. Fun
5. Social contact
6. Level of accomplishment
7. Emotions
8. Prolonged consequences
9. Probability
10. Chance
11. Coincidence
12. Surprise

We selected these dimensions on intuitive grounds, relying on lengthy discussions with over 100 gamblers. The stories were scaled by another group of 200 subjects, students at the University of Tilburg. All subjects judged two different stories, one representing chance, the other representing luck, which means that each story was judged by five students. The written instructions requested the subjects to first read both stories, then they were asked to judge the extent to which the concept represented by each scale applied to the story. The lay-out of the scales was like this:

surprise |----|----|----|----|----|----|----|

    not   totally

applicable   applicable

Dimensional Analysis

A discriminant analysis resulted in 68 correct classifications of stories. Seven chance stories were misclassified as luck stories, five luck stories were misclassified as chance stories. The discriminant equation consisted of a weighted linear combination of the 12 dimension scores. The correlations between the canonical discriminant function and the individual variables are presented in Table 7.2.

The statistical significance of the classification is expressed by the canonical correlation. The value of $r = 0.70$ implies that the classification was much better than could be expected if chance and luck stories did not really differ ($p < 0.01$).

The responses were also subjected to a factor analysis. The two factors extracted explained 30.3% and 16.69% of the variance. The factor loadings of the 12 dimensions are presented in Fig. 7.2.

The figure reveals two groups of aspects. One, related to chance, includes coincidence, surprise, fun and social contact. The group related to luck includes level of achievement, escape from negative consequences, important and prolonged

TABLE 7.2
Correlations Between Canonical Discriminant
Function and Individual Variables[a]

Dimension	Weight
2. Luck	0.56
3. Escape from negative consequences	0.56
1. Important consequences	0.51
6. Level of accomplishment	0.39
8. Prolonged consequences	0.18
7. Emotions	0.04
9. Probability	−0.04
5. Social contact	−0.27
4. Fun	−0.31
12. Surprise	−0.39
10. Chance	−0.40
11. Coincidence	−0.50

[a]Positive weights are indicative of luck, negative weights are indicative of chance.

consequences. Emotions had little relation to either group. Probability was not related to either group, presumably because many subjects gave a high rating when a story was highly *im*probable. Apparently the term was too ambiguous.

We may conclude that chance and luck are different concepts. People are able to produce stories that contain more of one concept than of the other, and they recognise these intended concepts in each other's stories. Both the discriminant analysis and the factor analysis reveal that chance is related to surprising coincidences, while luck is more related to an unexpected positive result, such as escape from misery or delivery of a difficult achievement. Since chance and luck were also themselves among the scaling dimensions, the relations between these concepts and the other dimensions are established doubly. It is not only true that chance and luck stories can be distinguished on the basis of a weighted combination of dimensional ratings, but also that chance and luck as rating scales are grouped within different subsets of the dimensional set.

A COVER STORIES STUDY

The nature of the previous experiment was exploratory. The outcome should be translated into predictions which are tested in a subsequent experiment, preferably utilising a different paradigm. Therefore I will formulate two predictions that lend themselves for further testing:

   a. When the surprisingness of an outcome is varied people will perceive this as a change in the influence of *chance* rather than *luck*.

   b. When the consequence of an outcome is varied people will perceive this as a change in the influence of *luck* rather than *chance*.

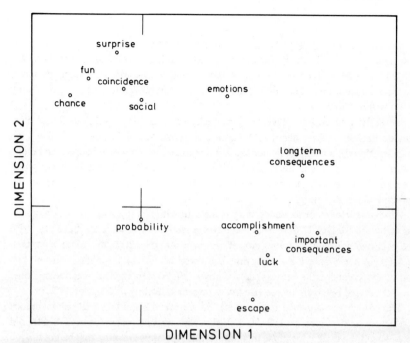

FIG. 7.2   Results of Princals analysis: position of 12 judgement scales in the plane
defined by the first two dimensions.

These predictions are tested in the following experiment. The idea is to construct pairs
of cover stories. The only difference between the members of a pair is related to the
surprise or the consequence of the event. Such pairs will be called *surprise pairs* and
consequence pairs. Subjects will be asked to judge the extent to which the event can
be attributed to luck or chance. A third type of pair, called *superstition pairs*, was added
to answer the question of whether superstitious acts (like touching wood) affect the
influence of chance or luck.

Story Construction

The stories were constructed by the experimenters, with the explicit objective of
representing a low or a high level of one of the three factors, surprise, consequence or
superstition. All stories were written with a high and a low level of the factor they were
representing, and with a positive and a negative outcome. Thus the four versions for
surprise stories were obtained by factorial combination of low and high surprise with
positive and negative outcomes. Consider the following example: "Tom Witkamp is
employed as a technician in a large international company, manufacturing timing
equipment. One out of the 100 technicians in his department will be sent to the Olympic
Games in Seoul, to assist with the timing of the sports events. Since each of the 100
would like to go to the games, they decide to draw lots. Tom wins, and is allowed to
experience the big event from nearby."

The low surprise version of the story was obtained by reduction of the number of colleagues to three. The negative outcome was introduced by explaining that one out of 100 (or three) colleagues is sent during the holiday season to an emergency job in the German Ruhr-area. They draw lots, Tom loses, and his family is leaving for sunny Spain without him.

Three more surprise plots were constructed, again each in four versions. These plots told of Emmy meeting her neighbour in a supermarket in France (or in her own neighbourhood); a stamp collector finding a valuable stamp which happens to be one out of the two missing in his collection (or one out of 100); and a family hearing that their house is the only one out of 120, that was not destroyed by a hurricane (or the only one out of three).

An example of a consequence story is the following:"Ann Van Dam bought a new car last week for Dfl. 22,000. The next day she read in the newspaper that a price rise had occurred unexpectedly: the price of her car went up by 20%, due to tax increases. By making her choice at the right time she saved herself 4400 guilders!" In the low consequence version the car was replaced by a Dfl. 70 camera. The negative outcome was introduced by changing the rise into a price cut, leading to a loss of 20%.

Three other consequence stories related how Barend acquired an all risk insurance just before he damaged his Dfl. 50,000 Mercedes beyond repair (or his Dfl. 800 old Fiat); how John caught his plane in a miraculous way, thus ensuring that he got the job he needed so dearly (or was on time for a dull meeting); and how Ricky's wallet was stolen just before his employer paid him his monthly wage of Dfl. 1,200 (or his afternoon wage Dfl. 12).

An example of a superstition story is the following: "Ingrid Wall is a psychology major at Leiden University. She is a good student, but experiences some problems with statistics. She was desperate about the final test, and she did not feel that additional study would do any good. Therefore she decided to learn the exercises in the course book by heart. The date for the test was fixed for February 18th, but at the last moment Ingrid had a feeling that it would go wrong on the 18th, and that she should delay the test. She feigned an illness, and was allowed to take a re-test on February 25th. You can imagine how much she congratulated herself when she discovered that on the 18th none of the problems were like the ones in the course book, whereas on the 25th three of the four problems were almost identical to the exercises she had crammed."

The low level of superstitious reasoning was achieved by saying that Ingrid was ill on the 18th and was forced to take the test on the 25th. The negative outcome was introduced by saying that on the 25th none of the problems were like the ones in the text book, whereas on the 18th three out of four were almost identical.

The other three superstition stories recounted how Eddy picked the only box office that had a concert ticket left, just by reasoning that three would be his lucky number [1] (or because box three happened to be opposite the tube exit); how Joyce met with little

---

[1] The Dutch expression is "Three times is the law of the sea", which does not contain a reference to luck.

competition in the Olympics selection contest in Amersfoort which she picked instead of Hengelo, because her dad and her mum were both born in Amersfoort (or because Amersfoort was closer); and how Tony happened to pick the only road that was not blocked by snow, by taking the one that reminded him of some happy childhood memories (or without any specific reasoning).

Method

A total of 385 subjects, students from various Dutch universities, participated in the experiment. Each of them read six different stories, all with positive outcomes or all with negative outcomes. Within the set of six stories the order was always: superstition, surprise, consequence, superstition, surprise consequence. The two stories containing the same factor were, of course, different, and the set represented both the high and low level of each factor. The subjects were instructed first to read all six stories. Then half of the subjects were asked to rate the extent to which the event was accounted for by chance. They responded by placing a check mark on a scale of 21cm in length. The scale looked like this:

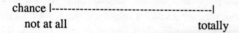

chance |--|
     not at all   totally

The other half of the subjects was asked to rate the extent to which the event was accounted for by good luck (for positive outcomes) or bad luck (for negative outcomes). The reason that these two labels were used is that in Dutch there is no neutral term referring to luck, irrespective of the result being good or bad.

Results

The scores were expressed in centimetres along the rating scales. The experiment was designed to test the prediction that variation of surprise and consequences would affect the perceived contributions of chance and luck differentially. Therefore the differences of scores at high and low levels of these conditions are considered. All entries in Table 7.3 are positive, which means that judgements of contributions of chance and luck were always larger at high levels of surprise, consequences and superstition. A high level of *surprise* significantly increased both the amount of perceived chance and luck. A high level of *consequence* affected only the amount of perceived luck. A high level of *superstitious reasoning* affected only the amount of perceived chance. This means that the predictions were only partly borne out by the data. Chance appeared to be related to surprise, whereas luck was more related to consequence. Additionally, however, increase of surprise also influenced the degree to which luck accounted for the events. The 95% confidence intervals for the total results in Table 7.3 indicate that the results can be summarised in the term of a somewhat weaker statement: surprise is more related to chance than to luck, consequences are more related to luck than to chance.

TABLE 7.3

Differences Between Stories at High and Low Levels of Surprise, Consequences and Superstition

Condition	Surprise	Consequence	Superstition
Luck			
Positive	2.82^b (1.04)	0.82 (1.13)	0.65 (1.04)
Negative	1.87^a (1.31)	2.04^a (1.17)	0.45 (1.24)
Total	2.34^b (0.85)	1.44^a (0.81)	0.54 (0.84)
Chance			
Positive	4.44^b (1.03)	1.05 (1.12)	1.89^a (1.08)
Negative	5.25^b (1.12)	0.08 (1.21)	1.21 (1.33)
Total	4.84^b (0.76)	0.58 (0.83)	1.56^a (0.88)

Note: The superscripts indicate significant outcomes of t-tests ($^a p < 0.01; ^b p < 0.001$). The bracketed numbers are 95% confidence intervals that extend to both sides of the means.

The effect of adding superstitious reasoning was that the outcome seems to be more caused by chance. That is, the outcome looked more like a coincidence, more surprising. It is obvious that superstitious reasoning does not change consequences; hence there is no reason why it should affect the contribution of luck. But, if superstition is related to chance at all, one would expect that doing things like touching wood or relying on lucky numbers would *decrease* the chance aspect of positive outcomes because the good result can now be attributed to the superstitious act. For negative outcomes the chance aspect should be increased, because the bad result came out, despite the superstitious act. The data show that the chance aspect of outcomes was increased significantly, both for positive and negative outcomes. This would be compatible with the notion that people do not rely on superstition, and that they are surprised when it has any effect at all. Another explanation of our finding is that inclusion of a superstitious act de-emphasises contribution of skill in the stories, which, in turn, would underscore the chance element.

Naturally the differences between high and low levels of each factor are small, relative to the maximum of 21. The reason is that people do not perceive the story outcomes as resulting from chance and luck only. There are always more circumscript causal factors that account for the outcomes to a considerable degree. Given that high and low levels of the same story were always judged by different groups of subjects it is, in itself, a surprise that these comparisons between subjects resulted in so many highly significant effects.

The overall pattern of results confirms that in the minds of people chance and luck account for the occurrence of events in different ways, and that they are related to different aspects of events. This dissociation can in the mind of a gambler create simultaneously an awareness of the statistical rules that govern the game, and a belief in personal good or bad luck. Big prizes come to them, not by chance, but through luck. Even if chance favours the house, then still luck may channel big prizes to individual players. In lotteries with a few big prizes there is no statistical law prohibiting anyone from winning those prizes. On the contrary, it is certain that some people will win them. But who the winner will be is a matter of luck.

RANDOMISERS AND CHOICE

The notion that luck would determine the outcome of the roulette wheel or the throw of dice is a bit confusing, because it implies that a sequence of such outcomes may show local alterations from what is to be expected by chance. To a physicist the idea of chance being modulated by personal luck may even be unacceptable. However, it should be realised that the outcome of a gamble is the result of a coincidence between a choice made by the gambler and a random event, beyond the gambler's control. If one wins at roulette, this is the result of the two events: the player selected a number, and the roulette wheel produced the same number. From my discussions with gamblers I learned that most do not, in fact, believe that they can influence the roulette wheel. Neither that luck will influence the roulette wheel or any other randomising device. But luck may influence the player's choice. The chance outcome of the roulette wheel is the same for all players, but betting is not. Good luck may help one player to bet on the right number, whilst as a result of bad luck other players bet on the wrong number. In this manner the concept of luck does not run counter to a purely physical explanation of how randomisers like roulette wheels, dice, and cards work. But belief in luck makes all reasoning based on the physical definition of a game irrelevant. Statistical rules, based on the assumption that in roulette all numbers are equally probable, a notion which is, in turn, derived from the physical construction of roulette wheels, only apply to the numbers that are produced. Analysis of the roulette wheel does not yield any information as to how players select their bets. This could explain why players are not discouraged by simple statements about the negative odds of a gamble. They do not expect that the wheel or the cards will turn in their favour. But they expect that luck will help them to select the correct bet. The remarkable owner of lottery ticket no. 1431, introduced in Chapter 1, kept his ticket because "It is all in the drum," by which was meant that the numbers which are drawn, are selected by a physical process that is not influenced by the identity of the ticket-holders. However, Mr. Luckwickel believed that ticket no. 1431 would be lucky for him and for no one else. Number 1431 will or will not win a prize; the outcome is uncertain. But gamblers should at least play their own part as well as possible. For him the best would be to own ticket no. 1431, because of the strictly personal meaning of this number. Such a personal meaning does not exist for others; when they keep the ticket this would be a suboptimal utilisation of luck. If a lucky person owns no. 1431 this must mean that 1431 will win. There is no causal relationship, only inference. If an unlucky person owns no. 1431 it means that 1431 will not win. It is like predicting the weather: when migrating birds leave it will soon freeze. But nobody earnestly believes that their departure causes the frost. It is just the reverse: the approaching frost makes the birds leave. In the same manner players expect that the prize on number 1431 causes the lucky gambler to own the corresponding ticket. What processes are involved in this retroactive causation is not exactly clear, but the subjective experience of luck inducing one to make the right choices is too strong to let people be worried by this problem. The Luckwichel paradox involves a reversal of causation in time, but so does the concept of luck itself. The basic fallacy of gamblers could well be a belief in luck, that is, a belief that through luck future outcomes may determine their choices.

CHAPTER 8

Theoretical Explanations

The primary paradox of gambling is that gamblers gamble and lose. For habitual gamblers the loss is certain, though not continuous: once in a while they win, but never enough to stay ahead of the house. Why don't they stop? Some explanations that look obvious at first sight do, in fact, even complicate the paradox instead of resolving it. One of these explanations is that gamblers engage in gambling as an innocent pastime, and that the amusement is worth the investment. The truth is that gamblers do not generally consider amusement more important than winning (cf. Chapter 3). Another explanation is that gamblers like to lose. This could be true for a small and rather sick minority of people, not for the vast numbers that engage in gambling regularly. The study of motives presented in Chapter 3 also contradicts this explanation: blackjack players pay attention to the expected value of a gamble, and appreciate a positive increase. Hence the "like to lose" issue complicates the paradox: gamblers continue to gamble and to lose, even though they want to win, and hate losing. Another simplistic explanation is that gamblers hope to make up for their losses in one extremely lucky coup. This could definitely be true for people playing in lotteries or football pools, since a small investment in these gambles can, in principle, produce an enormous yield, independently of the gamblers' strategy. But the chosen strategies in casino games like roulette and blackjack exclude the option of winning large amounts. In the game of blackjack, players refuse to spend a little time in the acquisition of essential skills. In roulette it was observed that players place their bets such that large deviations from the expected 2.7% loss are virtually impossible. The "hope" explanation adds again to the paradox: gamblers continue to gamble and to lose, they want to win and hate losing, but they prefer strategies that will never change their fate. I propose to abandon these

103

explanations, and to look at some deeper insights provided by the theoretical contexts, discussed in Chapter 1.

EXPLANATIONS FROM NORMATIVE THEORY

Normative theories like the Subjectively Expected Utility (SEU) model have primarily a prescriptive meaning: they tell us what to do if we want to maximise an outcome parameter. When people deviate from this prescription we could in principle accept the conclusion that people are not maximising that outcome parameter. The reason could be that the outcome parameter is wrongly chosen. Not considering the amount of effort spent at maximising could be one of the problems. When saving effort is included in the outcome definition, we could still maintain that people are maximising. In this way the maximisation of some outcome parameter may become an axiom; it is the investigator's task to model an outcome such that maximisation is preserved. The resulting theory is normative only within the restrictions imposed by the investigator. Simon (1957) talked about "bounded rationality" in this context.

Restrictions proposed by defenders of SEU theory are, in the first place, related to the transformation of monetary value into utility. A simple account of a preference for gambling would be a utility function that weighs losses less than wins. Assume, for instance, a player who weighs losses with a factor 0.5. A simple bet of size b on the red numbers in roulette would then result in an expected utility of 18/37 times b, minus 19/37 times 1/2 b, which equals 17/74 b. This positive utility should render the gamble attractive. The simple transformation does not account for the certainty effect and other phenomena reported in Chapter 1, which led to the conclusion that the utility curve must be concave for profits, and convex for losses. On the basis of the same observations it can be concluded that losses receive more weight than profits, which is in contradiction to the first explanation presented above. Such utility functions do, however, produce risk-averse preferences. In order to predict a preference for gambling a further adaptation is needed, such as a local deviation from concavity (the so-called Freedman-Savage utility curve, cf. Vlek & Wagenaar, 1979) or an overestimation of small probabilities.

A good example of a detailed normative theory, moulded by observations on real people, is Kahneman's and Tversky's *Prospect Theory* (1979). The basic deviations from strict application of the expected value principle are a non-linear utility curve of money, a non-linear relation between objective and subjective probability, and an editing operation that frames the decision problem in the context of future prospects relative to a present state. All these deviations were introduced with the intention of saving the rationality principle. In doing this, a certain degree of circularity has crept in. It is postulated that people overestimate small probabilities, because otherwise there is no explanation of why people buy lottery tickets. On the other hand, buying lottery tickets is supposed to be explained by the overestimation of small probabilities.

Of course Prospect Theory was also designed to predict other phenomena, not used for its construction. Hence Prospect Theory could be acceptable as an effective procedure, which is a procedure that transforms the stimulus conditions into behaviour (Johnson-Laird, 1983). But there are other doubts about the status of Prospect Theory as an effective procedure. The gambling paradox provides a perfect illustration. The acceptance of gambles with a negative expected value can be understood when it is assumed that small probabilities are overestimated. But it must also be explained why people prolong this overestimation after the experience of systematic losses. A key element of Prospect Theory is the adoption or exclusion of past experience in the status quo. It was demonstrated that compound bets are not integrated into one bet, such as assumed in Von Neumann's and Morgenstern's Axiom 6 (cf. Chapter 1). Prospect Theory accounts for this phenomenon by assuming that the second stage is considered after inclusion of stage one in the status quo. That is, stage two constitutes a new bet which is only considered after nullification of the previous outcome. In this way Prospect Theory could assume that gamblers simply discount all previous losses. This is refuted, however, by results presented in Chapters 2 and 4, because there it was shown that players incorporate previous wins and losses in their present strategies. Incorporation of previous outcomes is, on the other hand, sometimes assumed by Prospect Theory. "Consider a person who spent an afternoon at the race track, has already lost $140, and is considering a $10 bet on a 15 to 1 long shot in the last race. This decision can be framed in two ways, which correspond to two natural reference points. If the status quo is the reference point, the outcomes of the bet are framed as a gain of $140 and a loss of $10. On the other hand, it may be more natural to view the present state as a loss of $140 for the betting day, and accordingly frame the last bet as a chance to return to the reference point or to increase the loss to $150" (Tversky & Kahneman, 1981). The first implies, according to Prospect Theory, the acceptance of a risky bet, whereas the long shot is not particularly risky within the second frame. Gamblers who do not continuously adjust their reference point as they gamble, will, therefore, in the end accept bets that initially were judged unacceptable. This prediction is supported by McGlothin's observation that long shots are most popular on the last race of the day (McGlothin, 1956). But when players do not immediately nullify previous losses, it is hard to understand why they do not learn to adjust their probability estimates. By rendering the inclusion of previous outcomes as optional, Prospect Theory loses its power as an effective procedure. Which previous outcomes are included? None? The day's? The year's? All? A further concern is that, unlike the race track example, many bets cannot be construed as a possible way of making up for all previous losses, simply because they are too conservative. It is always possible to limit consideration of previous losses such that they can be compensated for by winning the next bet. But this again introduces the circularity that obstructs the use of the theory as an effective procedure.

The partition of series of gambles into separate bets which are considered singly is also not confirmed in a study in which repetition of identical bets was compared to playing the same bets only once (Keren & Wagenaar, 1987). Consider the option of receiving Dfl. 100 with 99% certainty, or Dfl. 250 with 50% certainty. When offered this unique choice, 67% of our subjects preferred the almost certain outcome, thus violating the expected value principle. However, when they were offered a choice between the same gambles, repeated ten times, 65% of our subjects preferred the risky gamble. This reversal demonstrates that people are able to consider sequences of gambles as a whole.

The conclusion of this discussion is that Prospect Theory, although it may account for incidental gambling, does not explain why people continue to gamble for years, despite their losses. The assumptions that are needed to account for prolonged gambling are that people do not learn to adjust their system parameters, and that past gambles are fully discounted, or that the prospect does always include the option of making up for previous losses. These assumptions are not tenable in the light of the observations presented throughout this book.

The inability to account for sustained gambling is not the only problem of Prospect Theory. Another one is the manner in which risk attitudes are dealt with. Prospect Theory allows for individual differences with respect to risk taking, but localises these differences in the relationship between value and utility, and between subjective and objective probability. People are predicted to be risk seeking when a combination of subjective probabilities and utilities leads them to prefer a gamble above its expected value. But this does not reflect a positive utility of risk, and the utility of risk itself is not entered into the equation. Prospect Theory does not incorporate individual preferences for risk as such, which is a major defect when gambling is involved, since running risks could be an objective of habitual gamblers.

Prospect Theory is not an effective procedure, it does not include a positive utility of risk, but worst of all, it does not explain all those strategies discussed in Chapters 2, 3 and 4: conservatism in hitting and doubling, insuring good hands, variation of bets, increase and decrease of risk in roulette, and many more. The reasoning underlying these strategies, such as belief in own skills or in the influence of luck, cannot be a part of Prospect Theory, simply because Prospect Theory does not assume reasoning. The only top-down element of Prospect Theory is the "editing" of the problem, resulting in a representation of alternative prospects, defined relative to the status quo. The transformation of probabilities and values are bottom-up processes, driven by stimulus values and unaffected by reasoning. Even when Prospect Theory explains *why* people gamble, it can still not explain *how* they gamble. But reasoning is very much at the heart of gambling. Understanding how people gamble is the key to understanding why they gamble at all. The reasoning that makes gamblers believe that a particular bet is favourable, is a sufficient account for the fact that they gamble. When people believe that 24 will be the winning number, there is no need to explain betting on 24 by risk propensity, overestimation of probabilities, or concave utility functions. The heuristics and biases tradition has evolved from the analysis of how people behave in specific situations. Would the total set of all these heuristics provide the reason why gamblers gamble?

EXPLANATIONS FROM HEURISTICS AND BIASES

In the study of everyday decision making no coherent alternative for normative theories has been proposed. Instead we have ended up with a "bag of tricks" called heuristics and biases. A long inventory of these was published by Hogarth (1981). I will first list a number of these reasoning strategies, which are also encountered in gambling. Almost by necessity some of the examples have an anecdotal nature, just like in Henslin's paper on the belief in magic in the game of craps (Henslin, 1967). In many cases, however, I will refer to the results discussed in previous chapters, or to interviews with a larger group of players (cf. Keren & Wagenaar, 1985). Almost all of the heuristics are described in detail in a collection of classical papers, edited by Kahneman, Slovic and Tversky (1982). Therefore no further references to these papers will be made in the present text.

Availability.   The ease with which specific instances can be recalled from memory, affects probability judgements. This can happen when the winners of lotteries and pools are well-publicised, or when winning in a gambling hall filled with slot machines is made very conspicuous. In a more subtle way the retrieval of memories of instances of winning might be enhanced because these are pleasant memories. Wagenaar (1986) reported in a study of autobiographical memory across a time span of six years, that it is much more difficult to retrieve unpleasant memories. In studies on the origins of compulsive gambling, Moran (1970), Custer (1982) and Lesieur and Custer (1984) noted that many compulsive gamblers first got into the habit of gambling after a long sequence of wins, which resulted in a considerable profit. Throughout the subsequent years this memory remained. In fact these people seem to believe that winning is the rule, whereas losing is only a temporary disturbance. In a study by Gilovich (1983) it was shown that betters in football pools remember their losses better than their wins, presumably because they spend more time reasoning these losses away. This does somewhat invalidate the availability explanation, but it must be realised that the recall of losses as if they could have been avoided, is less alarming and unpleasant than the recall of losses that are supposed to happen again.

Problem Framing.   The context in which a problem is framed determines the choice of strategy. This goes much further than the "editing" process assumed by Prospect Theory. Interviews with blackjack players revealed that many of them view the game as a team sport. The seven players sitting at the table are supposed to beat the dealer in a co-operative effort. When all of them stick together, they can do it. If one of them defects, the chances will reduce. If two defect there is no chance of winning. This belief is confirmed by the massive agreement with the statement that "A bad player can spoil the game for everyone" (cf. Table 3.1). The effect of this frame is not only that blackjack players may attribute their losses to others, but also that they try to find tables with better players, or that they insist on playing at private tables. One player told me that years ago winning was no problem at all, because players were very skilled. Since then gambling had become much more popular, and the majority of these new gamblers do not know how to play. Consequently losing had become the rule. Such players fail to identify their true opponent, viz. the negative odds of the game. Therefore they fail also to adopt strategies that help to improve the odds, like Basic, or card counting. The illusion of a match between players and dealer is encouraged by expert dealers, who attempt to create the atmosphere of a "good fight." Many players object less to losing after they had a good fight, because it offers the excuse that the dealer was too strong. The illusion is also shared by some pit bosses. They have a tendency to change dealers rapidly when the house is losing, as if bringing in "fresh" dealers would wear out the players.

Another example of problem framing is the insurance option in blackjack. Because the option is called "insurance" people construe a relation between the insurance bet (will the dealer's second card be a ten-value card?) and the original gamble (will the player end with a better total than the dealer?). People feel that a good total needs to be insured, because property is specially insured when it is precious. In reality, insurance has an expected value of $-1/13$ times the insurance bet, unless you are a card counter, and should therefore be avoided at all times.

A last example of problem framing is the custom of displaying the numbers that have come out on a roulette table. When there is no electronic display, players are provided with forms on which they can keep their own record. The emphasis on previous numbers puts roulette in the perspective of a problem solving task. The problem is to discover how future numbers can be predicted on the basis of previous numbers. The effect is again that players attribute their losses to a lack of skill, not to the odds that will not change, no matter how much experience they accumulate.

Confirmation Bias.   People seek information that is consistent with their own views, and discount disconfirming information. I encountered the strongest example of this bias in a professional blackjack dealer who, as a pastime, played blackjack. Asked how he could hope to win both as a dealer and as a player, he explained that the whole secret is in knowing the order of the cards in the deck. He had discovered that two successive cards add up to 10, 11 or 12: after a six comes a five, after a two comes an eight. When I expressed some disbelief, he took me to the blackjack table, and indeed, his rule was confirmed frequently. A quick computation shows that about one-quarter of the possible pairs confirm the rule, whereas three-quarters do not. A professional dealer deals about three million cards in a year. This dealer discarded over two million disconfirmations a year, and was even prepared to bet money on the result. Asked about his winnings he admitted that there were none. But this he attributed to the problem that there were not enough low cards to match the many picture cards that have a value of 10.

The heuristic proposed by this dealer is an example of neglecting regression to the mean. In general people expect that extreme values of a variable will be perpetuated.

One expects that extremely bright people will also have extremely bright children, as if intelligence is only a matter of superdominant genetic factors. When chance factors are interfering one is struck by the observation that extremely bright people have surprisingly mediocre children; and that extremely small mothers have children of a surprisingly normal size. The surprise reflects the belief that regression to the mean cannot occur by chance. Consequently one perceives regression to the mean as an extra force, causing alternation. The same can happen when sequences of cards are considered. If there is no "genetic" factor that creates a relation between successive cards, the chances are 11 to 2 that a 2 is followed by a higher card, 8 to 5 that a 10-value card is followed by a lower card. When these alternations are not expected, an illusion of systematic alternation is created, simply by the fact that a chance ordering enforces regression to the mean. However, this regression does, in no way, increase the predictability of the order of cards in a deck. Regression to the mean presents itself as a basis for prediction because it is confirmed so often.

Another example of confirmation bias is the roulette player who suddenly places a large single bet on number 24, completely out of his routine betting pattern. His reason was that 12 is always followed by 24. Twelve had come out previously, therefore he was quite certain that 24 would come next. After he lost his bet I enquired what had gone wrong. He said: "It almost worked." The number that did come out was 16, which is adjacent to 24 on the number wheel. Probably he would have considered other outcomes like 5, 10 and 33 also confirmations, because they are nearby on the wheel. Also he could have taken the outcomes 22, 23, 25 and 26 as confirmations because the numerical value is close. Or the numbers 20, 21, 26 and 27, because they are adjacent on the tableau. Thus 13 out of 37 possible outcomes could be taken as confirmations of a rule that has no predictive value whatsoever. We can add to this number all the occasions on which 24 or another confirmatory number occurred, not immediately, but in the second round. When the disconfirmations are neglected it is probable that such unfounded beliefs stick. Strong evidence for biased confirmation in gambling was provided by Gilovich (1983). He found that people predicting the outcome of football games spent more time in discussing their losses than their wins. What they tried to do was to find reasons for their mistakes. A content analysis of these discussions showed that losses were perceived as wrong outcomes, i.e. as outcomes that for some unexpected reason did not conform to an otherwise correct prediction. Thus the losses were not interpreted as a disproof of their prediction models. Discussions on wins tended to stress the fact that the outcomes proved the correctness of the prediction strategy. The extra time and effort spent discussing losses also led to a better recall of losses. This would contradict the availability explanation presented above.

Fixation on Absolute Frequency.   Absolute rather than relative frequency is used as a measure of success. I once placed an advertisement inviting people, who felt they had an unusual degree of luck, to contact me. One person claimed that he always won in lotteries, football pools, and the like. In the last year he had won a total of Dfl. 60,000. This was a really surprising feat, since he had accumulated the money through a large number of small prizes. Apparently he was winning quite often. However, when asked about how much he had spent at buying lottery tickets, he admitted that the total amounted to Dfl. 100,000. In fact he had lost more than he had won, but he discounted the losses, emphasising that the absolute number of times he had won was incredibly large. The same bias would work out disastrously when applied in the casino, because the odds in favour of the house are only slight. The frequent winning in roulette and blackjack would convince such players that they are blessed by an extraordinary amount of luck.

Concrete Information Bias.   Concrete information, such as that based on vivid memories or conspicuous incidents, dominates abstract information, such as computations or statistical data. In a study on the usage of seat belts (Wagenaar & Keren, 1986) we found that statistical information about the increased safety through use of seat belts is discarded by people, because they feel that statistics do not apply to their own individual case: "I am different, I drive safely." The same people were much more impressed by a newspaper clipping, telling how a girl from their own neighbourhood had died because she did not wear a seat belt. I have interviewed many blackjack players about the use of Basic and card counting. They invariably said that the general prescriptions of such systems could not work, because they neglect the idiosyncrasies of each specific situation. One player told me: "Listen, I have seen one of those card counters play. He lost his very first bet!" Players have trouble understanding the probabilistic nature of a strategy, based on statistical principles. They feel that an effective strategy ought to be effective in every single instance. Incidents like a roulette table paying large amounts to almost all players for a considerable time, are more likely to influence the gamblers' behaviour than the statistical reasoning demonstrating the superiority of Basic.

Concrete information bias could be the major obstacle for application of normative theories, such as the ones based on expected utility. Normative theories always involve long-term considerations. The application of the concept of expected value is extremely difficult in the unique case, in which the expected value is not even a possible outcome. The expected value of a bet on number 36 in roulette is -1/37 times the bet. The possible outcomes are -1 or +35 times the bet. What does the expected value mean if one plays only one round? In a study on unique versus repeated gambles (Keren & Wagenaar, 1987) we were able to demonstrate that people find it much easier to follow the prescriptions of normative theory, once they have adopted the perspective of repeated gambles. Confronted with unique gambles, aspects other than expected value seem to guide the decisions.

Concrete information bias could also be reflected in the use of probabilities. A long lasting discussion on the use of probabilities by individual decision makers has resulted in the position that people could have personal probabilities, which are more like degrees of belief. There is no reason why these personal beliefs could not be entered in the computation of expected utilities, as long as they conform to certain axioms. The interesting question is, of course, how these degrees of belief originate. The probability that 24 will be the next outcome of the roulette wheel could be based on statistical considerations, on observed relative frequencies, or on a whole number of other incidental observations. Concrete information bias would cause people to base their probability estimates on incidents, rather than on relative frequencies or statistical principles. The observed incident of another player winning a large prize might have a stronger impact than the normative consideration that the expected value of a gamble is negative.

Illusory Correlation.   Variables that, according to some stereotyped ideas, are related, seem to covary when in fact they do not. Illusory correlation is the basis of much superstition in sports and gambling. In The Netherlands, a football team won twice in succession while the local priest was present. Subsequently the team refused to play without their priest, and the poor man felt obliged to accompany the team for all its matches. Gamblers develop similar superstitions, related to lucky days, lucky dealers, lucky tables, lucky dresses, and so on. Strong examples of superstitious beliefs in the game of craps, founded on illusory correlation, are presented by Henslin (1967).

Superstitions could be quite harmless in the context of gambling behaviour, because often one decision is as good as the other. But it should be understood that such beliefs cause people to discard statistical probabilities. They may believe that, on the average, players lose more than they win, and still be convinced that the rule does not apply in their case, because today is their lucky day.

Inconsistency of Processing.   People are sometimes unable to apply a consistent judgemental strategy over a series of cases. When two conflicting prediction models are used as alternatives for each other, it is possible to create the illusion that outcomes are predictable, irrespective of what they are. When deciding to hit or stand at 15 points against a dealer's ace, players might consider the cards that have come out recently. Using the representativeness heuristic they will expect a high card after a number of low cards, and therefore decide to stand. They could also invoke the prescription of Basic, which is to hit. Now they are always able to interpret the result as a confirmation of one of the models, whatever the result is. A high card confirms a model that concerns the order of cards in the deck. A low card confirms a model that is based on long-term probabilistic considerations. Switching from one frame to the other causes one to believe that outcomes are predictable. Players often sigh: "I could have known it," in cases in which, in fact, they could not have known. The switching of judgemental strategies also facilitates the hindsight bias discussed further on.

Non-linear Extrapolation.   It is difficult to estimate joint probabilities of simple events. Any player can understand that betting on red or black in roulette results in a winning probability of almost 50%. It is, however, extremely difficult to estimate joint probabilities such as those presented in Fig.4.4. The chances after 100 or 1000 rounds of playing are hardly realities for players, even when they intend to play that many rounds.

Reliance on Habits.   People choose alternatives because it is customary to do so. In roulette some strong examples are found of preferred betting patterns, such as "Five, sixteen & neighbours," "The five numbers," and "The magic diamonds." These preferences are based on habit rather than on computation. But it looks very professional when a player instructs the croupier to place bets on "The seventeen neighbours." The experience of acquiring more and more complicated betting patterns may lull players into the suggestion that they are learning something that is relevant to the outcome of the game.

The somewhat surprising negative reaction to the offer of blackjack paying three times instead of one-and-a-half (Table 3.2) can be taken as another example of maintaining strong habits against reason.

Representativeness.   The judgement of the likelihood of an event is made by estimating its similarity to the class of which the event is supposed to be an exemplar. The likelihood of winning exactly five times out of ten, when the overall probability of winning is 50%, is overestimated, because an even distribution is a property of the population. A special form of this heuristic is the law of small numbers, which is the belief that small samples reflect the characteristics of the population from which they are drawn. Thus, in blackjack, people expect that the probability of winning is increased after three successive losses, a belief that is sometimes called the gambler's fallacy. The law of small numbers creates an expected dependency between successive events that are in principle independent. Roulette players believe that certain numbers are due, when they have not come up for a long time. Slot machines are felt to be "hot," when they do not pay the jackpot for a long time. The betting system of D'Alembert (cf. Chapter 4) is also based upon this belief.

In blackjack one can often see players bet on two or more adjacent boxes. Interviewed about this, 21 out of 28 players argued that one box "defends" the other. What they mean is that nature will balance the bad outcome on one box with a good outcome on the other box. A special way of betting on two boxes is to wager a low bet on the first box, and a high bet on the second. This allows the player to buy the bad cards on the first box, while directing the good cards to the second box. This strategy is based on the belief that there is a degree of dependence between successive cards, allowing a prediction of the value of the next card in the deck. The same belief is displayed in connection with the player on the seventh box (cf. Chapter 3): players on the seventh box are supposed to sacrifice themselves, and hit or stand when the next card is expected to be good or bad for the dealer.

The strongest effect of representativeness is found at the origin of the luck concept (cf. Chapter 7). Since players do not expect long runs of wins or losses, they perceive good and bad luck as the cause of these runs. The conviction that good and bad luck last for a certain period of time changes the perceived nature of the game considerably. Instead of seeing the game as determined by fixed odds, they now feel that their task is the detection of good and bad luck. In this manner losses will be attributed to lack of skill, rather than to adverse odds. Consequently players can always assure themselves that next time they will be more alert. In this way the representativeness principle prevents gamblers from ever learning.

Justifiability.   A justifiable rule is preferred over a rule for which no justification can be given. Some prescriptions of Basic are hard to justify in the light of direct evidence. With 16 points against a dealer's seven, one is required to hit, although the probability of busting is 8/13. The reason is that the probability of losing with 16 points is still higher. The justification of avoiding a bust is much more accessible, because the calculation is simple. A calculation of the probability of losing with 16 points against a seven is virtually impossible. Figure 2.2 shows that 90% of the players prefer the immediately justifiable action. Similar effects occur with players' low totals against a dealer's bad upcard. With 12 points against a dealer's four, the probability of busting after a hit is only 4/13. Still one should stand, since the probability that the dealer will bust is greater.

Reduction of Complexity.   Complex decision problems must be reduced to simple ones before a decision can be made. A good example of this heuristic is found in lotteries. Usually an extremely complex structure of prizes and successive draws ("classes") is set up, that even baffles the statistician at first sight. The purpose of this complex structure is to make the large value of some prizes, and the large total number of prizes, very conspicuous. It is hoped that these quantities enter into the gambler's decision structure, and that the small number of large prizes, the low value of most prizes, and the vast number of lottery tickets are discarded. The cascade structure of class lotteries, allowing one to play in succeeding draws when nothing is won thusfar, complicates the problem considerably. Most lotteries do not even advertise how many tickets are being sold, or what is done with unsold tickets, simply because gamblers do not even attempt to process that sort of information. The simultaneous existence of lotteries with vastly differing expected values illustrates this inability to analyse complex decision problems. People tend to accept lotteries when the price of a ticket is about right, when the size and the number of prizes are about right, but without consideration of the relation between these quantities.

Illusion of Control.   Activity concerning an uncertain outcome can by itself induce in a person feelings of control over the uncertain outcome. Again this is a mechanism most expertly employed by the designers of casino games. Roulette and blackjack are designed such that players must make decisions all the time. In blackjack these decisions do affect the expected value, although never to such an extent that the odds are against the house (excepting card counters). In roulette the decisions have no effect on the expected value of the game. People like this feeling of influencing the outcome; many blackjack players agreed with the statement that blackjack is to be preferred over roulette, because it provides greater control of the game (Table 3.2). Leaving a large number of decisions in the hands of the players, allows players to blame their own skill instead of the odds. Some gambles, such as football pools and betting on horses, suggest a large influence of skill. Even the Stock Exchange could be an example of this type. In reality the effect of skill is small or non-existent. Illusion of control is the condition for the occurrence of other heuristics, such as the belief that numbers in roulette can be predicted on the basis of previous outcomes, or the reliance on detection of good luck.

Biased Learning Structures.   Observed   outcomes   may   yield   incomplete information concerning predictive relationships. When blackjack players adopt the strategy of hitting on 12 points against a dealer's four, they will tend to record only the number of times that they won or lost through hitting. Thus they will come to the conclusion that winning is the more frequent outcome. They may fail to analyse what the result of standing would have been. More generally they may evaluate the effects of gambling, while bypassing the effects of not gambling.

Flexible Attribution.   There is a tendency to attribute successes to one's own skill, and failures to other influences. This bias, in a way, contradicts the illusion of control, which predicts that all outcomes are attributed to one's own skills. Flexible attribution could be one of the reasons why blackjack players are conservative, i.e. stand rather than hit. In this manner they succeed in avoiding an immediate bust, which should be attributed to their own decision to hit. When later on the dealer achieves a better total, they can attribute this to chance, bad luck or the dealer's skills.

Hindsight Bias.   In retrospect, people are not surprised about what has happened, and even believe that they did predict the outcome. Hindsight bias is a fundamental obstacle to learning. When it is believed that adverse outcomes were foreseen, or could have been foreseen, it is also believed that they will be foreseen in the future; that presentiments will be available, and therefore, that the absence of presentiments means that nothing bad will happen. But hindsight is, as a matter of principle, not available in advance, and cannot be used as a presentiment. Gamblers engage frequently in explaining why they lost, what went wrong, and why they could have known. This observation is supported by Gilovich's study on football pools (cf. the earlier section on confirmation bias). Blackjack players agreed massively with the statement that the quality of a decision can only be determined after the result is known (Table 3.1). For a player following Basic, or any other system, the quality of a decision depends on whether it is in accordance with the system, which can by judged in advance. No systematic learning can ever occur if decisions followed by winning are judged to be good, and vice versa.

COMPARISON OF NORMATIVE THEORY
AND HEURISTICS AND BIASES

Here I end the long but incomplete enumeration of heuristics and biases found in the literature. The heuristics and biases context is attractive, because many observations fit in it so well. It is, however, no more an effective procedure than normative theory, because it does not specify rules telling us which heuristic will be applied in a given situation. Even worse, from the individual differences among gamblers it is obvious that several heuristics could be chosen in one and the same situation, and that these heuristics lead to opposite behaviours. Thus the context of heuristics and biases will not allow us to predict actual choices made by individual gamblers. Experimental demonstrations of heuristics and biases never did yield unanimity among subjects, and explanation of the individual differences was rarely attempted.

Without exception the heuristics described above have the effect of reducing uncertainty. Gamblers are fighting the negative odds of games, specified by the rules, and they should attribute their losses to the odds embodied in dice, cards and roulette wheels. The uncertainty introduced by randomising devices is structural and cannot be evaded, even when the randomising occurs through a mechanism like horse racing or another sports event. Heuristic reasoning, however, causes gamblers to underestimate the influence of chance. The outcomes are not attributed only to dice, cards and roulette wheels, but also to luck and skill. Clear examples are the portrayal of blackjack as a team effort against the dealer, and the idea that gamblers can detect streaks of luck. In a way one could argue that heuristics and biases replace aleatory reasoning by epistemic reasoning (Beach, Barnes, & Christensen-Szalanski, 1986). In aleatory reasoning one can only make inferences about probabilities that hold across a large class of events. There is no way to obtain more specific information concerning one single event, such as the next roulette outcome, or the next throw of a dice. In epistemic reasoning specific knowledge about the unique characteristics of one event is involved. This knowledge can be used to predict outcomes with more precision than the probabilistic statement that holds for a whole class. Heuristics and biases provide gamblers with insights of the epistemic type, thereby suggesting that they have specific knowledge, that helps to overcome the odds. Moreover the effect of heuristics like confirmation bias, fixation on absolute frequency, illusory correlation, illusion of control, biased learning structures, flexible attribution and hindsight bias, is that gamblers do not learn from past losses that the employed modes of epistemic reasoning are invalid.

Thus, the heuristics and biases context attributes the acceptance of unfavourable bets, and the prolongation of gambling despite heavy losses, to a change of the concept of the games. Normative theory, on the other hand, attempts to explain gambling without essentially changing the nature of the game. The overestimation of probabilities and the transformation of monetary value into utility do not provide an opportunity to attribute the outcomes to something else than the odds of the game. It is not clear, then, why practice and ever accumulating losses do not result in a more accurate perception of the odds.

Normative theory accounts for the incidental acceptance of unfavourable gambles, but not for prolonged or habitual gambling. Neither does it account for the multitude of systematic deviations from strategies that would be optimal even in the context of adapted normative theories such as a theory of subjectively expected utility, or prospect theory. Consequently normative theory cannot be accepted as an effective procedure.

Heuristics and biases do explain why people accept unfavourable gambles, and why they continue to do so, despite their losses. The heuristics and biases explanation of prolonged gambling is parsimonious in the sense that only one principle accounts for all paradoxes: the conceptualisation of gambling as a game in which the outcomes depend on decisions made by the players. The heuristics context also accounts for the various strategies employed by gamblers as a whole, or by individual gamblers. However, at the level of strategy selection and individual choices the heuristics and biases context lacks parsimony. There are so many heuristics, that it will be virtually impossible to find behaviours that cannot be accounted for. Consequently the predictive value of this context is no better than in the case of normative theory. The heuristics and biases context will never be an effective procedure, unless we specify rules that govern the selection of heuristics. The study of gambling behaviour has taught us that such rules should take into account individual notions, conceptions, and values, so that a separate network of heuristics can be specified for each individual.

The difference between the two explanatory contexts becomes more prominent when remedies against compulsive gambling are considered. Explanations on the basis of normative theory would lead to attempts at changing the perception of probability and of the utility curve, in order to make the gamblers more risk averse. The heuristics and biases explanations lead to an attempt to change the conceptualisation of the gambles. One would hope that a clearer insight in the statistical rules that govern the games, and in the very limited contribution of skill and luck, would help to make each individual bet look less attractive. The experience with therapy of compulsive gambling is scarce, and not well documented (cf. Lesieur, Blume, & Zoppa, 1986). But there are indications that a change of the gamblers' cognitions result in a longer lasting abstinence than other approaches (Fonteijn, 1985). Understanding the probabilistic nature of gambles in general, and the unfavourable odds of commercially offered gambles, is only a first step, and no guarantee against the compulsion. But the replacement of this understanding by ways of reasoning that render each individual bet an irresistable offer, is fatal.

All paradoxes of gambling behaviour are caused by cognitions that characterise normal everyday reasoning, in which they are applied successfully most of the time. But also in everyday life we have a large repertoire of cognitions to choose from. Protection from blundering is not achieved by reduction of the repertoire, but by the development of clever selection rules. Little is known about these selection rules, which was the reason why heuristics and biases cannot be used as an effective procedure. Gamblers gamble, not because they have a bigger repertoire of heuristics, but because they select heuristics at the wrong occasions. The gambling situation is deliberately designed to be different from everyday life. Gamblers fail to appreciate how crucial the difference is.

THE GAMBLING PARADOX

The biggest paradox of gambling is that gambling exists at all, and that so many people engage in it voluntarily, without consideration of the negative expected value. It is even more difficult to understand habitual or addicted gambling, because people frequently engaging in gambling should, on the basis of feedback, have a sufficient insight into the relative frequencies of winning and losing. Normative theories and adaptations thereof, are not able to explain that simple fact, because they involve a long-term perspective.

From our discussions with gamblers it has become abundantly clear that gamblers are generally aware of the negative long-term result. They know that they have lost more than they have won, and that it will be the same in the future. But they fail to apply these statistical considerations to the next round, the next hour, or the next night. A rich repertoire of heuristics, borrowed from real life, in which they are used with more success, gives them the suggestion that statistics do not apply in the next round, or the next hour. That they know the next outcome, or that they will be lucky the next hour.

This habit of isolating instances from the larger sets to which they belong, called epistemic reasoning by Beach, Barnes, and Christensen-Szalanski, could well be the normal way of reasoning about everyday events. The bulk of research on the use of heuristics and biases seems to illustrate that people do not apply probabilistic principles, and that they are reasonably good "intuitive statisticians" when statistical problems can be solved in a non-statistical way.

Application of perfectly normal modes of reasoning leads to disaster when applied to gambling. The reason is that epistemic reasoning cannot be used when outcomes are controlled by randomising devices. People find it difficult to appreciate the true nature of roulette wheels, dice, cards and the drawing of lots. The difficulty is made worse by the clever design of casino games and lotteries. Almost every detail of organised gambling seems to be designed for the promotion of epistemic reasoning. It is sad but not paradoxical that people fall for it. The happy side-effect is that psychologists can discover, in the millions of gamblers, a rich garden full of all those varieties of reasoning that are so cumbersome to study in the laboratory.

References

Abram, P. (1981). The play of the general public in Atlantic City Blackjack. Paper presented on the *Fifth National Conference on Gambling and Risk Taking*, Stateline, Nevada.

Allais, M. (1953). Le comportement de l'homme rationnel devant la risque: critique des postulats et axioms de l'école Américaine. *Econometrica, 21*, 503–546.

American Jurisprudence (1968). Second edition, Volume 38. Rochester, N.Y. The Lawyers Co-operative Publishing Company.

Baker, R.J., & Nelder, J.A. (1978). *The GLIM system generalized linear interactive modelling* (Release 3).Harpenden, England: Rothamsted Experimental Station.

Beach, L.R., Barnes, V.E., & Christensen-Szalanski, J.J.J. (1986). Beyond heuristics and biases: A contingency model of judgmental forecasting. *Journal of Forecasting, 5*, 143–157.

Bell, D.E. (1982). Regret in decision making under uncertainty. *Operations Research, 30*, 961–981.

Bergler, E. (1957). *The Psychology of Gambling*. New York: Hill & Wang.

Berkeley, D., & Humphreys, P. (1982). Structuring decision problems and the "bias heuristic." *Acta Psychologica, 50*, 201–252.

Bond, N.A., Jr. (1974). Basic strategy and expectation in casino blackjack. *Organizational Behavior and Human Performance, 12*, 413–428.

Braun, J.H. (1980). *How to play winning blackjack*. Chicago: Data House.

Carroll, L. (1883). Lawn tennis tournaments. The true method of assigning prizes with a proof of the fallacy of the present method. In *The Penguin Complete Lewis Carroll*, Harmondsworth: Penguin Books.

Cohen, J. (1960). *Chance, skill and luck: The psychology of guessing and gambling*. Baltimore: Penguin Books.

Cornish, D.B. (1977). *Gambling: A review of the literature and its implications for policy and research.* London: Her Majesty's Stationery Office.

Csikszentmihalyi, M., & Bennett, S. (1971). An exploratory model of play. *American Anthropologist, 73,* 45–58.

Custer, R.L. (1982). An overview of compulsive gambling. In P.A.Carone, S.F.Yoles, S.H.Kiefer, & L.Krinsky, (Eds.), *Addictive disorders update: Alcoholism, drug abuse, gambling.* New York: Human Sciences Press.

De Leeuw, J., & Van Rijckevorsel, I. (1979). Homals and Princals; some generalizations of principal components analysis. In *Proceedings of the 2nd International Symposium on Data Analysis and Informatics Amsterdam.* Amsterdam: North Holland.

Devereaux, E.C., Jr. (1968). Gambling in psychological and sociological perspective. *International Encyclopedia of the Social Sciences, 6,* 53–62.

Dixon, N. (1976). *On the psychology of military incompetence.* New York: Basic Books.

Epstein, R.A. (1967). *The theory of gambling and statistical logic.* New York: Academic Press.

Fokker, G.A. (1862). *Geschiedenis der Loterijen in de Nederlanden.* Amsterdam: Muller.

Fonteijn, W. (1985). Over de behandeling van excessief gokken. *Kwartaalschrift voor Directieve Therapie en Hypnose, 5,* 227–242.

Friedman, M., & Savage, L.J. (1948). The utility analysis of choices involving risk. *Journal of Political Economy, 56,* 279–304.

Gilovich, T. (1983). Biased evaluation and persistence in gambling. *Journal of Personality and Social Psychology, 44,* 1110–1126.

Griffin, P.A. (1979). *The theory of blackjack.* Las Vegas: Gamblers Book Club.

Heider, F. (1958). *The psychology of interpersonal relations.* New York: Wiley.

Henslin, J.M. (1967). Craps and magic. *American Journal of Sociology, 73,* 316–330.

Hess, H.F., & Diller, J.V. (1969). Motivation for gambling as revealed in the marketing methods of the legitimate gambling industry. *Psychological Reports, 25,* 19–27.

Hogarth, R. (1981). *Judgment and choice.* New York: Wiley.

Humble, L., & Cooper, L. (1980). *The world's greatest blackjack book.* New York: Doubleday.

Humphreys, P., Svenson, O., & Vári, A. (Eds.) (1983). *Analysing and Aiding Decision Processes.* Amsterdam: North-Holland.

Johnson-Laird, P. (1983). *Mental Models.* Cambridge: Cambridge University Press.

Kahneman, D., Slovic, P., & Tversky, A. (1982). *Judgement under uncertainty: Heuristics and biases.* Cambridge: Cambridge University Press.

Kahneman, D., & Tversky, A. (1972). Subjective probability: A judgment of representativeness. *Cognitive Psychology, 3,* 430–454.

Kahneman, D., & Tversky, A. (1979). Prospect theory: an analysis of decision under risk. *Econometrica, 47,* 263–291.

Keren, G., & Wagenaar, W.A. (1983). Assessment of the quality of blackjack players in the three casinos of the Nationale Stichting Casinospelen. *Institute for Perception Report,* IZF C-15.

Keren, G., & Wagenaar, W.A. (1985). On the psychology of playing blackjack: normative and descriptive considerations with implications for decision theory. *Journal of Experimental Psychology: General, 114,* 133–158.

Keren, G., & Wagenaar, W.A. (1987). Temporal aspects of probabilistic predictions. *Bulletin of the Psychonomic Society, 25,* 61–64.

Keren, G., & Wagenaar, W.A. (1987). Violation of utility theory in unique and repeated gambles. *Journal of Experimental Psychology: Learning, Memory, and Cognition, 13,* 387–391.

Keren, G., Wagenaar, W.A., & Krul, A.J. (1982). Preliminary study on measures reducing advantages for system players in blackjack. *Institute for Perception Report,* IZF C-8.

Langer, E.J. (1975). The illusion of control. *Journal of Personality and Social Psychology, 32,* 311–328.

Lesieur, H.R., Blume, S.B., & Zoppa, R.M. (1986). Alcoholism, drug abuse and gambling. *Alcoholism, Clinical and Experimental Research, 10,* 33–38.

Lesieur, H.R., & Custer, R.L. (1984). Pathological gambling: roots, phases, and treatment. *Annals of American Academy of Political and Social Sciences, 474,* 146–156.

Lopes, L. (1981). Decision making in the short run. *Journal of Experimental Psychology: Human Learning and Memory, 7,* 377–385.

McGlothin, W.H. (1956). Stability of choices among uncertain alternatives. *American Journal of Psychology, 69,* 604–615.

Moran, E. (1970). Gambling as a form of dependence. *British Journal of the Addictions, 64,* 425.

Nelder, J.A., & Wedderburn, R.W.M. (1972). Generalized linear models. *Journal of the Royal Statistical Society, 135(a),* 370–384.

Oldman, D. (1974). Chance and skill: A study of roulette. *Sociology, 8,* 407–426.

Revere, L. (1980) *Playing blackjack as a business.* Secaucus, N.J.: Lyle Stuart.

Simon, H. (1957). *Models of man: Social and rational.* New York: Wiley.

Slovic, P., Fischhoff, B., & Lichtenstein, S. (1982). Response mode, framing and information-processing effects in risk assessment. In R. Hogarth (Ed.), *New directions for methodology of social and behavioral science: Question framing and response consistency (No. 11).* San Francisco: Jossey-Bass.

Solomon, H. (1966). Jurimetrics. In F.N. David (Ed.), *Research Papers in Statistics.* New York: Wiley

State of Montana ex. Dussault vs. Kilburn (1941). 111 *Mont* 400, 109 P2d 1113, 135 ALR 99.

Terheggen, E.H.M. (1980). 100 winnende zetten aan de roulette. Rijswijk, The Netherlands: Uitgeverij Elmar.

Thomas, W.I. (1901). The gaming instinct. *American Journal of Sociology, 6,* 750–763.

Thorp, E. (1966). *Beat the dealer.* New York: Vintage. Tversky, A., & Bar-Hillel, M. (1983). Risk: The long and the short. *Journal of Experimental Psychology: Learning, Memory, and Cognition, 9,* 713–717.

Tversky, A., & Kahneman, D. (1971). The belief in the "law of small numbers." *Psychological Bulletin, 76,* 105–110.

Tversky, A., & Kahneman, D. (1973). Availability: a heuristic for judging frequency and probability. *Cognitive Psychology, 5,* 207–232.

Tversky, A., & Kahneman, D. (1974). Judgment under uncertainty: heuristics and biases. *Science, 185,* 1124–1131.

Tversky, A., & Kahneman, D. (1981). The framing of decisions and the psychology of choice. *Science, 211,* 453–458.

Vickrey, W. (1945). Measuring marginal utility of reactions to risk. *Econometrica, 13,* 319–333.

Vlek, C.A.J., & Wagenaar, W.A. (1979). Judgement and decision under uncertainty. In J.A. Michon, E.G.J. Eijkman, & L.F.W. de Klerk (Eds.), *Handbook for Psychonomics*. Amsterdam: North-Holland, 253–345.

Von Neumann, J., & Morgenstern, O. (1944). *Theory of games and economic behavior*. Princeton: Princeton University Press. Reprinted (1964) New York: Wiley.

Wagenaar, W.A. (1970). Subjective randomness and the capacity to generate information. In A.F. Sanders (Ed.), *Attention and Performance III, Acta Psychologica, 33,* 233–242.

Wagenaar, W.A. (1972). *Sequential response bias: A study of choice and chance*. Rotterdam: Bronder-offset.

Wagenaar, W.A. (1986). My memory: A study of autobiographical memory over six years. *Cognitive Psychology, 18,* 225–252.

Wagenaar, W.A., & Keren, G. (1983). Money-flow at blackjack tables of three casinos. *Institute for Perception Report, IZF C-14.*

Wagenaar, W.A., & Keren, G. (1986). The seat belt paradox: Effect of adopted roles on information seeking. *Organizational Behavior and Human Decision Processes, 38,* 1–6.

Wagenaar, W.A., & Keren, G. (1988). Chance and luck are the same. *Journal of Behavioral Decision Making, 1,* 65–75.

Wagenaar, W.A., Keren, G., & Lichtenstein, S. (1988). Islanders and hostages: Deep and surface structures of decision problems. *Acta Psychologica, 67,* 175–189.

Wagenaar, W.A., Keren, G., & Pleit-Kuiper, A. (1984). The multiple objectives of gamblers. *Acta Psychologica, 56,* 167–178.

Wong, S. (1975). *Professional blackjack*. California: Pi Yee Press.

Yates, J.F., & Watts, R.A. (1975). Preference for deferred losses. *Organizational Behavior and Human Performance, 13,* 294–306.

Zola, I.K. (1963). Observations on gambling in a lower-class setting. *Social Problems, 10,* 353–361.

Author Index

Subject Index